data crush

how the information tidal wave is driving new business opportunities

CHRISTOPHER SURDAK

AMACOM AMERICAN MANAGEMENT ASSOCIATION
NEW YORK • ATLANTA • BRUSSELS • CHICAGO • MEXICO CITY
SAN FRANCISCO • SHANGHAI • TOKYO • TORONTO • WASHINGTON, D.C.

Bulk discounts available. For details visit:
www.amacombooks.org/go/specialsales
Or contact special sales:
Phone: 800-250-5308
Email: specialsls@amanet.org
View all the AMACOM titles at: www.amacombooks.org
American Management Association: www.amanet.org

This publication is designed to provide accurate and authoritative information in regard to the subject matter covered. It is sold with the understanding that the publisher is not engaged in rendering legal, accounting, or other professional service. If legal advice or other expert assistance is required, the services of a competent professional person should be sought.

Library of Congress Cataloging-in-Publication Data
Surdak, Christopher.
    Data crush : how the information tidal wave is driving new business opportunities / Christopher Surdak.
        pages cm
    Includes bibliographical references and index.
    ISBN-13: 978-0-8144-3374-4
    ISBN-10: 0-8144-3374-X
    1. Information technology—Management.   2. Marketing research—Data processing.   3. Business intelligence—Data processing.   4. Big data.   I. Title.
    HD30.2.S87 2014
    658.4'038—dc23   2013035087

About AMA

American Management Association (www.amanet.org) is a world leader in talent development, advancing the skills of individuals to drive business success. Our mission is to support the goals of individuals and organizations through a complete range of products and services, including classroom and virtual seminars, webcasts, webinars, podcasts, conferences, corporate and government solutions, business books, and research. AMA's approach to improving performance combines experiential learning—learning through doing—with opportunities for ongoing professional growth at every step of one's career journey.

Printing number
10 9 8 7 6 5 4 3 2 1

This book is dedicated to
my wife Jeanne and my daughter Ryleigh.
You are my motivation and inspiration,
and I appreciate your love and support.

I would also like to dedicate this book
to the memory of my friend and colleague
Thomas Bookwalter Sr.
Thomas had a tremendous, positive impact upon
everyone he met, and we lost him far too soon.

CONTENTS

FOREWORD

As President and CEO of the Association of Information and Image Management (AIIM), I get the chance to interact with thousands of information management experts on a daily basis. AIIM is a key resource for its more than 100,000 members, who are at the forefront of the struggle to manage information sprawl.

In this role, I've worked with Chris Surdak for several years, including coauthoring an ebook on social media and collaboration management. Through these interactions, it is clear that Chris has deep experience with the challenges of managing data and information in our daily lives, while trying to maintain some semblance of control.

A range of market forces are bringing dramatic changes in our world, including mobility, cloud computing, social media, and online commerce. While each of these forces is a powerful driver of both data growth and business change, it is their interdependence and mutual feedbacks that will truly transform the business landscape. Collectively, they are bringing about changes in our world that will impact nearly every aspect of global business.

Both companies and individuals will be affected by these changes, and it is critical to understand what the new business environment will look like and what might be your place in it. Part of this understanding is to ensure that your business remains relevant in a world awash in digital devices and the data that they create; part of this understanding is to figure out new ways to thrive in this world through transforming both your organization and yourself.

In *Data Crush*, Surdak provides specific insights into what the future of our deeply connected, highly digitized world will look like and what needs to be done to compete effectively in the near future. Chris discusses how data has become the currency of business and will be the basis of every effective business decision as the world grows more interconnected and complex.

For years, organizations have had systems and strategies for managing their money—their financial assets. They also usually have systems to manage their employees—their human assets. They often have ERP systems for managing their physical assets. But far too few organizations have systems and strategies for managing their most important assets in a digital world—their information assets. However, it is these information assets that will determine the future winners and losers in a global battle for the ever-shortening attention span of digitally addicted consumers.

I believe you'll find this book both entertaining and useful. I know that I did, and I find that the advice that the author provides can lessen the impact data overload will have on your sanity, and possibly, help keep your company on top of the data crush, instead of beneath it!

John Mancini, CEO, Association of Information
and Image Management (AIIM), March, 2013

INTRODUCTION

As a technology consultant, I am motivated to stay up-to-date on the latest and greatest new technologies and trends. During the past decade, I've come to recognize an undercurrent in the world of technology and the Internet, a force that was both an enabler of new technologies and a potential barrier to their advancement: data growth.

If you're like most "connected" people, you start your day by logging into one or more email accounts to see how your day is going to go. If you're an average person, you're wading through about 150 emails each day, trying to determine what deserves your attention and what can be deleted. Perhaps you've noticed that over the last decade the amount of email you get every day has been slowly and steadily increasing. You may also have noticed that many of these emails show that some third parties seem to know an awful lot about what you do or do not like, where you shop, where you eat, and so on.

Further, if you also work in or with information technology, you've probably noted that more and more of your work involves dealing with an ever-growing mountain of data. Regardless of what you do professionally, our world is becoming flooded with data—and the more we use it and depend upon it, the more we seem to generate.

Prepare to Be Crushed

My aim in *Data Crush* is to make some sense of this explosion of data in our world. We'll be looking at where all of this data growth comes from, what is driving it, the impacts that this growth will have on your business, and how business must respond to succeed in a world awash with information.

Six major trends are driving the growth and significance of online data for both individuals and organizations. As they converge upon and reinforce each other, they lead to increasingly complicated information management issues. The trends are:

1. **Mobility:** Smartphones and tablets keeping us connected all the time.

2. **Virtual Living:** Increasing interaction with our friends and family through the Internet.

3. **Digital Commerce:** Infinite options for buying goods and services online.

4. **Online Entertainment:** Billions of channels and millions of games to keep us entertained.

5. **Cloud Computing:** Placing all of our information "out there" in the ether.

6. **"Big Data":** The massive amounts of data created by our online activities.

Companies must deal with these six trends in every aspect of their operations. This "perfect storm" of converging demands leaves us very little margin for error in addressing the impact of these forces on our businesses, and almost every organization is struggling to balance these issues. Taken independently, each of these forces is driving dramatic, double-digit growth in the amount of data in our lives. However, these forces are not independent of one another. Rather, they are deeply interdependent; each one leveraging and enabling the others toward even greater data growth.

As a result of these interdependencies, the growth of data in our world is accelerating exponentially. In a 2012 study, networking powerhouse Cisco estimated that the world's yearly data traffic will reach 1.3 zettabytes by the year 2016.[1] To put this number into perspective, think of the capacity of a high-end laptop from 2013. It likely has a terabyte of storage, which is quite a bit for the individual user. That's enough space to store hundreds of movies, tens of thousands of music files, or millions of electronic photos.

By comparison, a zettabyte would be equal to a billion such laptop drives, which is no small number by any account. To put it in terms that further defy the imagination, if a zettabyte of data was burned onto data CDs, the resulting stack of CDs would be 4.1 million kilometers high. This is high enough to reach from the earth to the moon and back again more than five times. Hence, if you are a business person who feels overwhelmed by data here in 2013, I'm afraid that things are going to get much, much more challenging over the next decade or so.

New Challenges, New Opportunities

A Chinese proverb says that in any crisis lies opportunity, and the same is true of the data crush under which we find ourselves. By now you have likely heard the term "Big Data," which is the application of statistical analyses to the mountains of information that we have at our disposal. The goal is to gain new business insights. Therein lies the opportunity in the explosion of data; the ability to create a deep, rich understanding of our business and its customers. Indeed, companies that are early adopters of Big Data are finding dramatic improvements in their operational efficiency, customer satisfaction, and profitability. As we explore the impact of Big Data on contemporary business, you'll see why data analytics will be critical to business success in the immediate future.

My colleague John Mancini, CEO of the Association of Information and Image Management (AIIM), lists six imperatives that business leaders must follow to be successful in this new world. They are[2]:

- *Make Everything Mobile:* Redefine content delivery and process automation to take advantage of mobile devices and mobile workforces.

- *Digitize Processes:* Drive paper out of processes and automate process flows.

- *Make the Business Social:* Integrate social technologies into processes rather than creating stand-alone social networks.

- *Automate Information Governance:* Acknowledge that paper-based paradigms no longer work and focus on automating governance and disposition.

- *Mine Big Content:* Find insights and value in massive aggregations of unstructured information.

- *Commit to the Cloud:* Break down monolithic "enterprise" solutions into more "app-like" solutions that can be deployed quickly—independent of platform and in the cloud.

As you will soon see, these edicts closely align with the recommendations that I make in this book. This is not a coincidence. Rather, it is intended to be a call to action for all business people who wish to succeed in this new business environment.

Organization of *Data Crush*

Data Crush is organized into three primary sections, each made up of six chapters. First, we will review the six market forces mentioned above, looking at their individual rates of growth and the resulting impact on data growth that companies are experiencing. Second, we'll look at the six strategies that companies must adopt to respond to these forces. We will review maturity models for each strategy, so that you can determine how far your company has gone in adapting to changes in the marketplace. Finally, we will review six specific actions that your company can take right now to prepare for the future.

My goal through this journey is to both entertain and inform. The size of the business challenge that I will be presenting may seem a bit overwhelming, but I think you'll be motivated by the opportunities presented.

The book closes with a summary chapter that presents five scenarios of what life may be like in the year 2020 based on the trends presented in the chapters. These scenarios will provide a context for what all of these changes may lead to in the near future and will help identify some of the business opportunities that may present themselves as a result of our increasingly data-driven world.

I hope that these scenarios demonstrate that our data-enabled world will be a great place to live and work. True, we will have to be open to revealing more about ourselves than we desire, but the benefits will make us more and more likely to opt in to this datafied world rather than become digital luddites living at the fringe of the information age. With that, let's dive right in and prepare to be crushed.

part one

what's driving the data crush?

A range of social forces has both grown from and feeds into the availability of information in our world. It is no longer news to anyone that social media, mobile phones, ecommerce, digital entertainment, cloud computing, and Big Data are life-changing technologies. However, in this part I hope to achieve a few goals. First, I want to qualify each of these six social and technical trends, explaining what are they about, how they impact our lives, and how they contribute to data growth. Second, I want to quantify each topic by describing their rates of adoption and growth and their future trends. Finally, I intend to demonstrate how each of these trends is impacting the evolution of multiple industries. Thus, this part should help you put each trend into context with your work and your life, so that you can understand how each is driving the changes that you're experiencing every day.

With that, let's dive into the recent past, so that we can better understand the near future.

1

mobility
smartphones, tablets, and the "internet of things"

AS OF 2013, if you're a typical American, there's about a 60 percent chance that you've got a smartphone in your purse or pocket.[1] You use it to tweet with colleagues, shop for goods, take photos, and make videos to share with friends. Perhaps you use this same device to play games while you're waiting in line to buy a coffee at a store that you found on Google maps. You may be using an electronic coupon sent to you by an "app" that you recently downloaded, based upon recommendations from some of your "friends" on Facebook. And, you may synchronize this smartphone with your home computer, work laptop, and spouse's smartphone using a cloud computing service.

It's a pretty remarkable thought that all these activities were unheard of just a decade ago. Indeed, it wasn't that long ago that people used their cell phones just to talk to one another. Today, cell phones are bringing dramatic shifts to every aspect of our lives. In fact, according to Google, one in seven online searches now originates from a mobile device and 72 percent of smartphone owners use their phones to enhance their shopping experiences.[2]

Mobile computing, made possible with smartphones, is perhaps the fastest growing and most prolific form of technology in human history. In terms of adoption, mobility is right up there with the creation of fire and electricity. In 2010, 4.5 billion people worldwide owned a mobile phone.[3] Remarkably, in that same year, only 4.2 billion people owned toothbrushes.[4] In 2012, between 1.5 and 1.7 billion phones were sold worldwide, meaning that one-fifth of the total human population bought a new phone that year. And, by 2013, the number of mobile users had grown to over 6.8 billion,[5] or almost 90 percent of all humanity. Indeed, mobile phones are no longer a luxury. Rather, they are an individual's dominant point of interaction with the modern world; an item that is so critical to our lives that we'll forego other needs to stay connected.

Mobile phones are so deeply integrated into our day-to-day lives that it's hard to imagine a world without them. As a result of this level of adoption, the market for mobile communications now represents $1.3 trillion, or approximately two percent,[6] of the world's Gross Domestic Product (GDP). And the growth of this market is far outpacing the growth of GDP in general.

Traditional cell phones (dumb phones, if you like) are still the majority of those in use throughout the world (approximately 70 percent of all phones), but smartphones are rapidly taking over the mobile market. While the total annual sales of mobile phones has seemed to peak due to market saturation, significant numbers of users are trading in traditional mobile phones for smartphones. Indeed, the market for smartphones has turned the mobile industry on its ear, with new players Apple and Google completely annihilating former stalwart mobile players, such as Nokia and Research in Motion (RIM).

Today, it's difficult to remember just how much Nokia and RIM dominated the mobile industry only a decade ago. In 2000, I was one of the millions of people caught up in the craze for the ultimate fashion-statement phone: the chrome-plated Nokia 8810. Although this "dumb phone" retailed for nearly $1,000, Nokia couldn't manufacture them fast enough. Even famous-for-being-famous celebrity Paris Hilton was an early adopter. And, of course, there was the Nokia 7110 with which Keanu Reeves costarred in the movie *The Matrix*.

Nokia saw its fortunes change as phones became smarter and users grew to care about function as much as form. Nokia invested a great deal of time and energy into expanding the functionality of its phones, but it seemed that the company was trying to take giant leaps by creating an entirely new operating system: Symbian. While users wanted more functionality (phones like the BlackBerry, which could send and read email), they didn't necessarily want to learn a whole new operating system to obtain this capability. As such, Symbian languished in obscurity, and few people bought into the big, heavy, and complex phones on which it ran.

As for RIM, its BlackBerry was the technological precursor to the smartphone, allowing users to access email as well as make calls and text. Again, the BlackBerry was a major fashion statement, and Paris Hilton quickly changed over to this new superphone. So addictive were the new capabilities of this phone, that it quickly gained the title of "Crackberry," after the highly addictive, cocaine-based street drug. The BlackBerry was THE phone to own as late as 2008, when presidential nominee Barack Obama refused to surrender his "Crackberry" to members of the Secret Service, despite their concerns over his privacy and security. The Crackberry was so addictive that in the early 2000s, I had a manager with whom you could not make eye contact during a discussion because he was so busy reading his email on his Crackberry.

Skip to the year 2012, and both Nokia and RIM are in deep trouble. RIM continues to press forward with an independent operating system on its phones, despite seeing its market share drop from a high of 44.5 percent in 2008 to a recent low of approximately 4.6 percent in 2012.[7] Nokia has been forced to largely abandon its own smartphone operating system and has cast its lot with Microsoft's Windows Mobile 8 operating system. Nevertheless, Nokia has seen its global market share plummet by over 25 percentage points in just a decade[8]—and this in a market that has tripled in size during the same period. Combined, these two companies have lost approximately $200 billion in market value in the last 10 years,[9] a dramatic loss in net worth caused by their failure to foresee the explosion of smartphones. The reasons for this massive upheaval in the mobile industry are both obvious and compelling. Smartphones can deeply enrich our lives at so many levels, and this transition reveals itself in looking at the growth of mobile data services, mobile apps, and location services.

Mobility and Data Growth

Which aspects of mobility are leading to the explosive growth in data volume? Four primary drivers of data growth are caused by mobility: pervasiveness, connectedness, data enablement, and context. Let's look at each of these drivers in turn.

First, there is pervasiveness, also known as the network effect. With more than six billion cell phone users on the planet right now, there is always someone you can talk to and always something to say. And, most of us take advantage of this pervasiveness all of the time.

For example, in the United States in 2012, 34 percent of homes no longer had a land line phone.[10] Rather, the inhabitants of these homes simply rely on their cells phones to remain connected to the world. Total voice service usage was over 2.3 trillion minutes in the United States in 2012[11] and was growing steadily at three percent year over year.[12]

Combining pervasiveness with the second driver, connectedness, means that whenever you might have something to say it is highly likely that someone is willing and able to listen, no matter how inane the conversation might be. Not only are nearly six billion people connected to the network, they are connected almost perpetually and can interact with other people 24 hours every day should they choose to do so. Perhaps you've noticed the impact of connectedness in your work life, where the old standard 9-to-5 workday has been replaced by a workday that seems endless. In my work, it is not uncommon to have teleconferences that begin at six in the morning (because I need to talk with people in Europe) and continue on into the evening (because I need to talk with people in Asia, who are just beginning their next work day). Because of my connectedness, I have far greater opportunities to generate more and more data.

The more than 2.3 trillion minutes of talk time that American mobile phones supported in 2012 translates to about 10 hours per month for every person.[13] So, it's safe to say that mobile phones are still used for voice communications. However, data communication has become increasingly important to users, as is shown by the over 2.27 trillion text messages Americans sent to each other in 2012.[14] Both text message and voice traffic are growing at about three percent per year, indicating that they have reached a point of saturation—at least for now. These forms of traffic are expected to continue to grow, albeit more slowly, as more and more users communicate with each other through social platforms like Twitter and Facebook.

Mobile Data Services

Data enablement of phones gets wrapped up in a discussion of mobile data services. One of the things that makes a smartphone "smart" is its ability to access data in a wide variety of forms. Mobile data services include text messages, web browsing, accessing apps, and streaming services such as Netflix and YouTube. As smartphones replace regular mobile phones and as cellular data networks expand their footprint across vast segments of China, India, and other developing countries, data services have rapidly replaced voice services as the dominant form of mobile traffic.

In contrast to voice and message traffic, data traffic grew by more than 100 percent in 2012, reaching 1.1 billion gigabytes of data.[15] Now that's a really big number, and a doubling of the rate of growth shows little evidence of slowing down. Rather, it is anticipated that this rate of growth will accelerate as more customers migrate to smartphones and more devices start to link into cellular networks. Smartphones have rapidly eclipsed traditional computers as points of entry for the Internet for the simple reason that we carry these devices with us nearly all of the time, allowing us to access the internet anytime, anywhere. This trend will continue to multiply as nonhuman users, or "things," plug in and start to communicate with us.

Data Enablement and the Age of the App

On March 2, 2012, Apple announced that it had reached 25 billion downloads of apps from its app store, a remarkable number given that the store didn't exist prior to July 2008. By early 2013, this number exceeded 40 billion downloads, a remarkable rate of growth.[16] As the app store reached its five-year anniversary, it offered more than 775,000 apps to its users and is adding several thousand more every week.[17] Not to be outdone, Goggle's app store for its Android operating system has posted similar numbers of apps and downloads, creating billions of dollars in revenue and revolutionizing the lives of billions of smartphone users worldwide.[17] Indeed, global revenue from apps is expected to rise a full 62 percent to $25 billion in 2013, according to Gartner, Inc.[18]

Given how popular "apps" are, I suspect you're at least familiar with them. But for the uninitiated, an app, or mobile app, is generally defined as a software application designed to operate on a mobile computing device, such as a smartphone or tablet. Apple, Google, and other platform sponsors provide similarly vague definitions, so I'd like to add to them by defining some key characteristics of successful apps:

1. **Apps are inexpensive to use:** A key to successful apps is a low barrier to entry. Not all apps are free, but most cost less than $10, and a majority are under $5.

2. **Apps take advantage of the mobile platform:** Apps are designed for use on smartphones and tablets, and therefore should take advantage of the unique benefits of these platforms. Namely, they can be used anywhere at any time by anyone who has a specific need. Beyond that, successful apps allow users to do things that they cannot readily do with a laptop or desktop computer, which means that the app takes advantage of the mobile platform.

3. **Apps meet a specific need:** Most successful apps fulfill a focused, specific user need. Whether the user is looking for five minutes of entertainment from a game app, the closest gas station, or someone nearby with whom to have lunch, apps should provide a valuable service to the user when and where that service is needed.

4. **Apps know their owner:** Apps that are really successful keep track of their users. This can be as simple as Angry Birds keeping track of your personal high scores or as complicated as an app knowing your favorite shopping or dining venues. The better a given app knows you, the more likely you are to use it. This creates a self-reinforcing relationship that makes some apps almost addictive to their users.

Other apps might have additional characteristics, but these four are the keys to an app's success. That many apps miss these marks is apparent when one realizes that of the over 750,000 apps in the Apple App Store, more than 400,000 have never been downloaded.[19] Given the 40 billion downloads that have taken place, it should also be apparent that successful apps are often wildly so. One need only consider the universal backlash against Apple when it dropped Google maps in favor of its in-house-developed iMaps in 2012 to realize that people take their apps personally!

Apps are relevant to this discussion of data growth because they are both consumers and creators of vast quantities of data. For example, apps that work off of a user's location generate data on that location every time the app is used. The creation of these time and date stamps, which was originally unknown to users and undisclosed by app creators, led to several high-profile scandals in 2010. While there was initially some backlash against Apple and Google for keeping and using these records for unknown purposes, users quickly got over their initial concerns and kept on downloading newer and more sophisticated apps, which tracked their activities even more closely. This aspect of apps will become more and more prevalent as they grow in sophistication and capability. Hence, they will generate an ever-growing torrent of information. In Chapter 10, we will return to the world of apps and how they are changing the way businesses will have to engage with their customers over the coming decade.

Location Services and Contextual Computing

The final driver of mobile data growth mentioned earlier is context. Context on mobile devices refers to a user's location in time and space; it leads to a wide range of apps that take advantage of a person's location in delivering content to a user. These location services, or contextual computing, further increase the value of smartphones, as seen by the steady growth of location-based services in Figure 1.1. Since the turn of the century most mobile phones have been able to tap into signals from the Global Positioning System (GPS), a constellation of satellites orbiting the earth that allows devices to determine their location in space and time with remarkable accuracy. Using this information, mobile phones can tell their users both where and "when" they are, otherwise known as location services. When you combine location services with the powers of a smartphone, you can create what is called contextual computing.

Contextual computing combines the where and when of a user with other relevant data available to a smartphone, thereby creating a result that is relevant to that user's particular when and where. A simple example is when you perform a search for "gas station" with a mapping application on a smartphone. Unless you enter another specific location, the results that are returned are those gas stations closest to your present position. If you don't specify otherwise, the app assumes that you're searching for gas stations closest to where you are, or your present context in the world. The unique combination of where you are, when you are timewise, and who you are creates nearly limitless opportunities to sell you something 24 hours

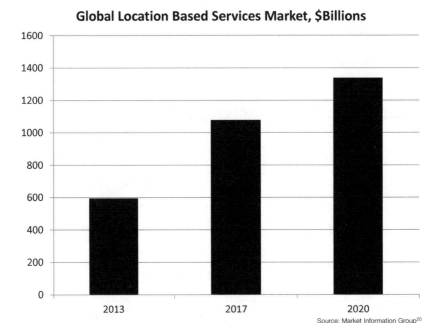

Global Location Based Services Market, $Billions

Source: Market Information Group[20]

FIGURE 1.1. Growth in Location-Based Services

a day. As such, contextual computing will create several orders of magnitude more data for each of us to create and consume.

Wearable Computing

By 2014, new, wearable computers should be available for consumers. Google released its Google Glass computer glasses in 2013, and the anticipated-yet-unconfirmed iGlasses from Apple cannot be far behind. These wearable computers allow users to experience "enhanced reality," in which digital information is projected into the user's field of view, displaying contextual data that are relevant to where the user is looking. For instance, if a wearer of these smart glasses is looking for a particular store, the directions to that store are projected into his or her field of view, obviating the need to constantly look down at the smartphone screen.

In addition, these smart glasses will be fitted with video cameras, which allow the user to create first-person videos (videos from the wearer's perspective) of experiences. These videos can then be shared with others, either through direct streaming to or through sharing on websites such as YouTube. Now, you might wonder just how much people want to experience each others' lives, but one need only look at the success of sites like Facebook, Twitter, and YouTube to forecast that smart glasses will be a game-changing technology. Just as smartphones have led to a one or two order of magnitude increase in the amount of data generated on the Internet, smart glasses will cause a similar jump in the amount of data created.

Further, the video feature of smart glasses will allow imaging to be added to the sources of data that feed contextual computing. As such, in the near future, the Jamba Juice app that you've downloaded to your iGlasses will know that you're currently out shopping with your friend Tom (facial recognition software run against the video file that you just posted to Facebook); that Tom loves Very Berry smoothies from Jamba Juice (comparison against Tom's prior purchasing behavior); and that you're both near your local Jamba Juice shop (location data from the iGlasses). Put all of these together, and the Jamba Juice app knows to text an offer to the two of you for a two-for-one discount at that Jamba Juice, if you both stop by in the next 15 minutes.

Smartglasses will further explode data growth. Consider this. If each person wearing smart glasses records five minutes out of every hour in the day, that's the equivalent of creating a feature-length film . . . every day. Assuming that smart glasses follow the same sort of adoption rates that we have seen with smartphones or tablets, it is reasonable to expect that by 2020 tens of millions of smart glasses will be in the hands of users. As such, it doesn't take a genius to figure out that YouTube is going to need a lot more storage capacity, and soon.

As this rudimentary example implies, the near future of mobility is going to generate a titanic amount of data and will also demand titanic amounts of computing power and network bandwidth. Successful companies will acknowledge these demands and will meet them—because economic survival will make these investments imperative.

The "Internet of Things"

While the market for mobile phones is rapidly approaching saturation, another market stands to make the mobile market appear vanishingly small. Known as the "Internet of Things," this market will consist of devices that are self-aware, user-aware, environment-aware, and most important, connected. These connected things will generate streams of data that will dwarf the volume of messages that our networks currently support. And, as these things get smarter and smarter and grow to understand their users more and more intimately, they will start to communicate with each other more and more frequently, without human intervention. Some analysts forecast that by 2020 things will be sending more messages to each other than they will to the users that they support.

Examples already exist, such as cars equipped with OnStar or televisions equipped with Wi-Fi connections. These bridgehead applications will rapidly be followed by an invasion of connected devices, including appliances, medical devices—and even clothing. Indeed, if we include the emerging world of radio frequency identity devices (RFID), nearly everything in our world will be able to communicate with everything else.

As stunning as the growth in mobile data volume may be, we haven't yet begun to experience truly large amounts of information flow in our society. This even though we're fast approaching a point of mobile saturation, where everyone who wants a cell phone has one. Does this mean that we will soon reach a peak in mobile data traffic? Hardly. Rather, the source of mobile data traffic will soon make a gigantic shift away from humans toward the objects in our lives. In the very near future, the bulk of mobile traffic will come from things rather than people. Smart cars, smart appliances, smart meters, and smart this and that all will be connected via mobile technology. Once connected, they will each create a steady stream of messages, notifying the world of their status, their availability, and so on. As the quantity of these smart devices begins to eclipse that of cell phones, we will begin to see a level of data communications and messaging that will dwarf the traffic levels of today. I call this market shift "thingification," and we'll address this phenomenon in depth in Chapter 12.

These four characteristics of mobility—pervasiveness, connectedness, data enablement, and context—will all continue to expand the availability and, hence, the consumption of vast quantities of information. These characteristics make mobile devices, such as smartphones, indispensable to their users, and so there is little chance that our addiction to our little pocket computers will ebb any time soon.

CHAPTER SUMMARY

1. Mobile technology has rapidly become pervasive across the globe, with nearly 90 percent of the world's population currently using some form of mobile device.

2. This pervasiveness has subsequently led to a dramatic increase in connectedness between people. More people are spending more time online, as can be seen by recent growth trends in the number of voice minutes, texts, and data consumption by mobile devices.

3. Data enablement of mobile devices is rapidly expanding around the globe and, indeed, mobile access to the Internet may exceed that by other connected devices by the year 2015.

4. Context services have been a key driver in mobility adoption and data growth, and yet are at their infancy. Contextual services will certainly experience double-digit annual growth rates over the coming decade and may overtake all other forms of data traffic on the Internet within that time frame.

2

virtual living
the rise and growing dominance
of social media

WHETHER YOU CALL IT social media, social computing, Web 2.0 or online living, this new form of Internet presence has transformed the daily life of nearly every person on the planet. Arguably, Web 2.0 has had more of an impact upon our society than even Web 1.0, and there is every indication that social media will continue to grow in both adoption across the human population and in ongoing use by those already plugged into these networks.

Let's look at this technology and social phenomenon by analyzing some of the most popular social platforms of the early 2010s.

Facebook
If you have been living under a rock since the middle of the 2000s, perhaps you have not heard of Facebook. Facebook is a social media

site that allows users to connect with each other online. Once connected, people can post messages on their personal online page; these messages are then shared with other people with whom the poster has connected. Users may respond to each other's posts either by clicking on a "like" button which indicated that a user happens to like the post or by responding with their own messages. In this way, Facebook has created an environment where millions of people can hold billions of conversations with each other. Facebook facilitates the creation of millions of "digital tribes," where members chit chat back and forth over an enormous range of topics.

A decade into the Facebook era, many of us find it hard to remember life before Facebook arrived on the scene. Today, Facebook and its voluble cousin, Twitter, have become global, cultural phenomena. In 2012, 1.06 billion people spent approximately 10.2 billion minutes per day on Facebook (excluding mobile users),[1] and average users each spend over 400 minutes per month logged into the site.[2] At the U.S.' Federal minimum wage of $7.25/hour, 10 billion minutes per day is equivalent to $450 billion of lost economic activity per year. That's a lot of wasted time when American businesses are facing one of the roughest economic periods in modern history.

By early 2013, Facebook had eclipsed the one billion user mark.[1] In fact, "Facebooking" is the second most popular web-based activity by click rate; the first is searching on Google. Facebook is the number one online activity by minutes spent, capturing around nine percent of all time spent online by all users.[3] As any frequent user of Facebook knows, it's very easy to drown in the message traffic on Facebook, especially if you use it on your smartphone.

Naturally, Facebook has invested billions of dollars on infrastructure to support this growth, which leads to the question of where this money comes from. As with most other "free" services on the

Internet, Facebook makes its revenues by selling the end-user data that it collects to third parties—both for targeted advertising on Facebook itself and for independent analysis by companies that wish to know more about their customers. What makes Facebook's data uniquely valuable to marketers is the level of personal intimacy displayed by Facebook users. For many, Facebook is treated as if it were a private phone call between friends rather than a publicly displayed and recorded interaction that can be subsequently analyzed by psychologists and their new best friends: data scientists.

Twitter

Facebook is not the only major player in the social media space. For those who are less verbose, there's Twitter. Twitter's operating model is somewhat different from that of Facebook's, and it is particularly well suited to mobile users. Users of Twitter create "tweets," which are short 140-character-long messages. Users publish these tweets to the whole world rather than just to a specific audience of approved friends, as with Facebook. Twitter users can subscribe to each other's tweets, allowing users to establish a following, of sorts. Further, most tweets are searchable by anyone, making the vast well of previously sent tweets available to others for analysis.

Not to be outdone by Facebook, Twitter has seen even greater rates of adoption over its very short lifespan. From its start in March 2006, Twitter's growth has been faster than, if not as large as, Facebook's. By 2012, Twitter signed up over 200 million active members worldwide.[4] This population of users, most of them mobile, send over 400 million tweets every day.[5] Further, because old tweets are retained and can be searched, Twitter also supports over 1.6 billion searches every day.[6] These searches are made both by individuals looking for specific information and by companies that are monitoring Twitter traffic for information of market. Indeed, Twitter's commercial model is to limit the amount of data that is provided for free and to charge fees to those who want to access the full Twitter data stream. Further, Twitter has built its advertising revenue in the same vein as Facebook, leveraging detailed profiling to target users with specific marketing messages.

Anyone doubting the power of Twitter as a social platform need only look at the number of subscribers that various celebrities have collected on the platform. Some stars with the greatest number of Twitter groupies include[7]:

- Justin Bieber: 36 million followers

- Lady Gaga: 35 million followers

- Katy Perry: 34 million followers

- Rihanna: 29 million followers

- President Obama: 28 million followers

Keep in mind that the population of California is approximately 37 million; so the great state of Bieber-followers is almost as large. These few examples illustrate just how much influence Twitter has as a platform and how much influence having a Twitter following may give you.

Business Impact of Social Media

What does all of this mean to companies? Why should businesses view social media as anything other than an extremely large chat room, where teenagers go to post questionable notes and pictures to one another? Social media is so much more than that, and it's not a stretch to call it a revolution in human communications. Love them or hate them, Facebook, Twitter, and other social media sites are transforming nearly every aspect of our world, including how people want and expect to interact with each other. This new expectation of casual intimacy on the part of social media users has extended beyond their immediate digital tribes and now includes the businesses with which they interact. Indeed, if your business is not taking advantage of this channel for customer engagement, you stand to lose a great deal of customer mind share, and wallet share, over the coming decade.

One of the challenges created for companies wanting to take advantage of social media is that these platforms have changed customer expectations of company engagement. Not even 10 years ago, engagement might have constituted giving a customer a discount on a product or service on a birthday. Engagement today means offering that same customer a discount on their friend's birthday, while knowing exactly what that friend would like as a gift based on his or her profile. Because of social media, engagement now implies a level of customer intimacy that borders on intrusive, as marketers are now able to profile customers to a frightening degree. However, by using this level of intimacy, companies are able to respond to customer needs with such depth that many customers cannot imagine *not* being taken advantage of in this way. The benefits users receive from social media are of such great value to them that, for many, the loss of privacy inherent in this customer intimacy is worth it.

The intimacy imperative necessarily means that your business must act differently than before. Now, when customers interact with your organization they expect that you know and understand them at a deep, personal level. When they call into your customer support center, they expect you to know everything about them: what they've bought from you in the past, what their issues might be, and most certainly how to solve their issues that very instant. In the past, companies bought, deployed, and relied on Customer Relationship

Management (CRM) systems to perform this task. These CRM systems kept track of customer interactions, included what they bought and when and if they called for support. They might also keep track of some customer-specific data, such as addresses and birthdates. By the early 2000s, this level of customer data was considered to be "customer intimacy." However, with social media we can achieve a level of customer intimacy that leaves CRM systems in the dust.

Through social media, a company is able to tap into a customer's feelings, attitudes, thoughts, fears, and desires. On these platforms, people reveal a tremendous amount of intimate information about themselves, almost ignoring the consequences of such openness. In return for revealing so much about themselves, customers may receive a range of benefits from companies eager to serve their needs. So, while people give up a great deal of privacy on social media, they can receive some significant benefits in return.

By the 2010s, if you didn't respond appropriately to these new expectations, the very next action that customers were likely to take was to flame your company on every social media platform to which they have access. The cycle time between a missed customer service opportunity and publication of the resulting bad reviews is now measured in seconds, particularly as more and more social media users move to mobile computing platforms and are perpetually connected to their tribes. Only those companies that successfully forecast and embrace these changes are likely to survive in the near future, as the social media idiom changes not only how companies deal with customers, but how the businesses themselves operate.

Risks and Rewards of Social Media

One side effect of the Facebook revolution is that a significant proportion of the human population is now living its life online. Frequent Facebook users seem to live every moment of their lives on the site, and there appears to be little or no concern over their personal privacy or the limits of basic decency. People seem to give little or no thought to what they post online, and most appear to click "send" without any concerns as to the consequences. Indeed, as early as 2010, 81 percent of divorce lawyers surveyed stated that Facebook was a significant source of evidence in their trials.[8]

By now you have almost certainly heard some of the horror stories of what people admit to on Facebook. Cases of fraud, theft, rape, and even murder have all been freely admitted to by users of Facebook, leading to disbelief by many of their Facebook friends and relatively easy prosecutions by district attorneys. It seems that cases such as these appear in the news on almost a weekly basis, and yet Facebook users continue to bare their collective souls to the world online. By 2010, so much incriminating information was available on social media platforms that most federal, state, and local law enforcement agencies actively troll these systems looking for evidence of foul play. When Edward Snowden "outed" the National Security Agency's surveillance program in 2013, the public response was fairly muted. It appears that the general public is now used to the idea that we are all under a microscope and that somehow the benefits outweigh the costs.

Social media facilitate the most intimate of discussions among users, who seem to forget that they're communicating on a public forum. Not only is such intimate communication normal on Facebook, it's almost expected by users. Why is this relevant? Because for companies to harvest the most value from social media, they too must appear to bare their souls to their customers—freely admitting when they have failed to meet customer expectations and publicly apologizing to customers who feel offended by their thoughtlessness. Communications such as this will be new and uncomfortable to most marketers, customer service executives, and nearly all corporate attorneys. However, this is the new normal in customer engagement, and the companies who figure out how to create and maintain this level of customer intimacy will be those who derive the most value from social media.

The Evolving Value of Social: What Makes Facebook Worth Billions of Dollars?

When Facebook went public in 2012, its market value peaked at $108 billion,[9] a nontrivial amount of money to be sure. At the time, it was the largest initial public offering for an Internet company. This begs the question: How could a company that provides a free service to its customers be worth so much money? To answer this question, I look to my favorite quotation from a venture capitalist: "If you aren't paying for it, then YOU are the product!" This is true of many "free" services on the Internet (think Google, Hotmail, or Yahoo), and it is particularly true of Facebook, which struggled to monetize its business to meet investor expectations (See Figure 2.1).

Facebook will meet its monetization goals by selling its information—your information—to companies that want to sell stuff to you. All of the posts that you put on Facebook help to paint a portrait of you. Who are your friends, what are your likes and dislikes, how intelligent are you, how educated are you, and what are your interests or hobbies? All of this information can easily be extracted from the constant flow of comments, pictures, and "likes" that users of Facebook place on the site every day. And, the more prolific a person is on Facebook, the deeper and more accurately they can be modeled, analyzed, and probed.

Further, Facebook uses a range of user-oriented games both to entertain and gain even deeper insights into the psyches of its users.

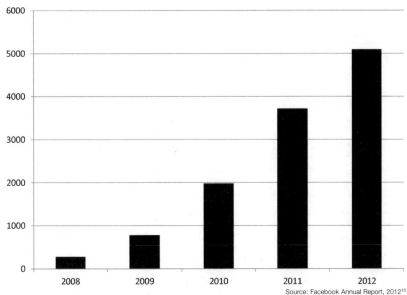

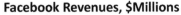

FIGURE 2.1. Facebook Revenues, 2008–2012

In fact, games can be particularly revealing as to a person's personality type, propensity to compete with others, sociability, and even IQ. If you're a Facebook user and have found yourself bombarded by friend requests inviting you to play games on Facebook, ask yourself why Facebook is working so hard to get you to play its games. I guarantee that a significant proportion of its motivation is that game playing provides a much more accurate picture of you as a user and a consumer, which Facebook can subsequently monetize by selling your profile to others.

What Facebook has to sell to companies is an intimate, accurate profile of tens of millions of people, all of whom can more readily be sold to using all of the information that they commit to their Facebook posts. Perhaps you've noticed this change in Facebook over the last couple of years. You're starting to get more advertising on your Facebook page, and those advertisements are probably more interesting to you than those presented on other websites. This is particularly true if you spend a lot of time on Facebook. The more time you spend on the site, the more advertisers learn about you and the more valuable your eyeballs become to them.

Transforming Social Media: From Customer Engagement to Customer Intimacy

Marketing is the business of reaching consumers' wallets by engaging with their hearts and minds. As such, the better you can understand a given customer's preferences, desires, attitudes, and needs, the more likely you are to sell them something. This, then, is ultimately the value of Facebook: Users are so deeply engaged with Facebook and share so much of themselves on the site that advertisers can profile each individual user to such an extent that they can target them with advertising that reaches each customer at a deep, fundamental level.

This necessarily means that marketers have had to change their approach from that of reaching as many people as possible with a universally attractive message to sending marketing messages that resonate specifically with individual people. Initially, this approach is more expensive and more complex, as this nearly infinite number of different messages must be created, organized, and appropriately delivered. Yet another example of data crush. However, once the necessary systems and content are in place, delivering these messages to the appropriate consumer at the appropriate time is trivial and, indeed, is part of the service provided by the platform owners (e.g., Facebook, Google).

Once a company is prepared to deal with every single customer as an individual and once that same company has access to a detailed profile of each customer, it can advance from mere customer engagement to customer intimacy. With customer intimacy, the company achieves a level of connection with the customer that is equal to that which best friends have with each other. Indeed, customer intimacy implies that the company has become a full-fledged member of the customer's digital tribe, establishing a level of trust that can lead to tremendous brand loyalty and, hence, profitability.

The Business of Social Media: Early Moves, Initial Results

By now, most companies have set up at least a rudimentary presence on Facebook. They own their company name as a Facebook domain, and they probably have a team of people in their marketing department who post to the site information that they believe may be relevant to their followers. Still others have taken additional steps in social media adoption, including creating dedicated apps, proactive engagement of customers on their own sites, and the creation and maintenance of customer blogs, which encourage online discussions among customers.

Given the importance of social media in the lives of hundreds of millions of people, embracing social media as a customer outreach channel is not merely an option. Regardless of the nature of your business, it is imperative that you embrace this new paradigm, just as surely as it was imperative to embrace the Internet back in the early 1990s. That revolution changed the world of business forever. The revolution brought about by social media will make the changes wrought by the Internet seem trivial by comparison.

CHAPTER SUMMARY

1. Social media has rapidly become the number one activity on the Internet, consuming over four trillion minutes of the population's time in 2014.[11]

2. While Twitter and Facebook are rapidly reaching market saturation, their user traffic is likely to continue its high double-digit growth rates into the foreseeable future.

3. Through social media, it is possible to model peoples' behaviors, beliefs, preferences, and opinions with a level of accuracy and relevancy that was previously impossible.

4. The rapidly growing revenue streams of leading social media platforms is evidence that companies are starting to leverage them as sources of customer data and for targeted advertising.

5. Because SOME companies are beginning to achieve customer intimacy through social platforms, customers will soon expect ALL companies to provide a similarly rich customer service experience.

3

digital commerce
infinite options for buying goods and services online

THE EXPLOSIVE data growth that everyone is experiencing infiltrates all aspects of our economy, society, and lives. As with any technology shift, there are both good and bad aspects to the changes that result, just as there are both business winners and losers from each generation of technology. In terms of the day-to-day experience of most people in the developed world, no segment has been more enabled by and challenged by the Internet than the world of retail. Data-enabled shopping has completely changed our purchasing experience, has undermined some of the greatest brand names of the 20th century, and has created some of the new-age brands that will dominate the 21st century.

When the Internet was born, so was digital commerce. Back in the late 1990s, consumers were introduced to such stalwart brands as Amazon.com and eBay. Back then, many pundits argued that these companies would never be able to compete with traditional retail chains because they could never match the "personal shopping experience."

A decade later, both Amazon and eBay have become the 800-pound gorillas of the retail world, and traditional retailers are now struggling to survive. Amazon.com's revenues tripled between 2009 and 2013 to over $60 billion,[1] while the list of traditional retailers nearing or entering bankruptcy grows deeper and deeper. Although most of these traditional retailers attempt to compete with Amazon and eBay with their own online presence, still other entrants onto the retail stage are shaking up the world's buying experience. Today, standard bearers such as Amazon.com are eating into every niche of retail, and new commerce players such as Groupon and Price Grabber are driving innovation in retail with instant coupons, real-time custom orders and price comparisons, virtual fitting rooms, and collective price bargaining. Consequently, traditional stores are finding it ever harder to stay in business. The bottom line, however, is that ongoing change will bring both new challenges and new opportunities for shoppers.

While the new features and functions provided by digital retailers are compelling, they will also further contribute to the data deluge that consumers are experiencing. Companies pay for these new features by exploiting the ever-deepening knowledge that they develop about how, why, and what customers shop for. Once the information is in their systems, they will inundate potential customers with new deals based on these insights. Indeed, the fact that some retailers are using detailed consumer data to optimize their marketing budgets means that retailers who aren't doing the same are quickly being put at a dramatic disadvantage. It is not enough to have this customer data and review it on a quarterly basis. Rather, retailers must use this data in real time to sell items to customers even before those purchases are needed.

The Polarization of Consumers: Ultrapremium Versus Commodity

One of the social trends that retail sales figures clearly show is a strong customer polarization through all segments of retail. Customer buying behavior is increasingly being driven to the ends of the price–value continuum, that is, customers are choosing to spend more, sometimes substantially more, for what they perceive to be high-quality brands (think Apple, Coach, Virgin Atlantic, or Mercedes-Benz). These brands have established themselves as purveyors of luxury goods or services, and they deliver a lifestyle or a statement about the purchaser. Subsequently, these companies are able to charge a premium for their products and services, and customers appear happy to pay these premiums in order to partake of the added value that they represent.

Conversely, some customers are also shopping purely on price and are demanding deep discounts from the companies who serve this end of the market (think Walmart, Costco, Southwest Airlines, or Kia). These companies succeed because inexpensiveness has a quality all its own, and customers appreciate that they can expand their buying power by meeting their basic needs at deep discounts, thereby freeing up funds for the occasional luxury purchase. These companies are successful because they are able to capture larger proportions of the available market, thus leveraging efficiencies of scale and scope to continue the downward pressure on the prices that they charge, while maintaining or even enhancing their own profits.

Walmart is certainly the dominant player in the commodity space and has become so formidable a retail channel that its 2012 revenues of over $470 billion represents over three percent of the total gross domestic product (GDP)[2] of the United States. In fact, Walmart's profit in 2012 of $15.7 billion[3] was almost equal to JC Penney's total revenue for the year ($17.26 billion).[4] Middle-tier retailers, like JCPenney, Sears, Kmart, and Macy's, are suffering dramatic erosion of store revenues, while their online channels are substantially less efficient than those of Amazon or Walmart. As such, these middle market players will continue their steep decline and, indeed, they may no longer exist by the year 2020.

The companies that serve what used to be the middle ground of the quality–price continuum are those that are getting left without a chair when the music stops and customers finally spend their money. The troubled companies mentioned in the previous section are a virtual membership list for the middle market, and they are quickly being made irrelevant by shoppers' ability to find and take advantage of open markets and near-perfect competition.

Certainly customers still shop in these stores, if for no other reason than to partake of shopping as a pleasurable, social activity. However, when these same shoppers are ready to buy, an ever-increasing proportion of them are leveraging mobile technology to perform an immediate price check on the item that they're ready to purchase. When this occurs, the retailer loses all of its pricing power, as well as all of the local-market advantages that it may have held by maintaining a retail location in the vicinity of that customer. As long as the shipping costs are manageable, that customer will more than likely find the item for sale more cheaply from an online source, and the middle-market retailer will lose the sale that it had facilitated through its investment in brick-and-mortar stores.

This insidious shifting of pricing power to the consumer will continue to erode middle-market companies' ability to differentiate themselves. Their profitability is too low to sell on their brand image or high-touch customer service, and their fixed and variable costs are too high to compete on price with the discount chains. Hence, these companies find themselves in a retail no-man's-land where few if any can survive over the coming decade.

The Collapse of Brick-and-Mortar Retail

It's no surprise that traditional retail has suffered mightily due to online competition. Recent victims of the decline of brick-and-mortar retail include Borders books, Blockbuster, Filene's, Ultimate Electronics, Metropark, and Super Fresh Foods. In additional, several other well-known retail brands are in deep financial trouble, including OfficeMax, Pacific Sunwear, RadioShack, Rite Aid, Sears, Kmart, Talbots, and JC Penney. These companies are seeing their in-store revenues in steep decline, while the costs to maintain these physical marketplaces continue to rise with inflation.

At the close of the 2012 holiday shopping season, a number of key midmarket retail chains had announced plans to close stores across the country, including Best Buy (closing between 20 and 25 percent of its stores), Sears (closing 5 to 6 percent of its stores), JC Penney (closing 30 to 35 percent of its stores), Office Depot (closing 10 to 12 percent of its stores), and Barnes & Noble (closing 30 to 40 percent of its stores).[5] Most of these companies have seen significant revenue erosion due to the shift of consumer dollars to online channels. And, they have experienced even more significant profit erosion due to shifting consumer pricing power created by those online channels.

Does all of this spell the end of the shopping mall? Hardly. While some traditional retailers are struggling to survive, others are thriving. What might explain this distinction between retail winners and retail losers? One word: data. Those retailers that combine the value of local, physical presence with the power of customer data are actually growing their revenues and profits despite the strength of online competition. These retailers understand the value of having a customer physically in their store ready to make a purchase, and they add to this all of the information that might be available about that customer. Smart retailers use their inherent advantage of the customer's presence to close the deal by intelligently applying the very same customer data that makes online buying so compelling. Put these two factors together, and retailers may experience a renaissance. Fail to embrace the power of customer context, and your business will continue to erode in the face of data-enabled competition.

New Sales Modes and Models

Traditional retailers can claim a strategic advantage over online retailers; they can provide customers with a real-life, first-person buying experience. These companies use their stores to allow customers to physically browse through merchandise, facilitating shopping as an activity or experience that people view as a pastime. No doubt there is some truth to this view of retail "shoppertainment," as many of us can admit to enjoying going to a store simply to shop around. Many traditional retailers discount the power of online retailers such as Amazon, because they cannot replicate the real-world shopping experience that is available at your local shopping mall.

However, providing this front-end of the consumption experience does not necessarily dictate that a store must operate in traditional ways. In fact, some new retailers are providing customers with a satisfying, on-premise shopping experience while competing their fulfillment in a very online sort of way. Take men's clothier

Bonobos. This chain provides consumers with retail locations where they can browse products, try on items to see how they fit and feel, and look at different materials and cuts. Once a customer's measurements and preferences are recorded, Bonobos uses this information to take orders from the customer. However, Bonobos customers do not actually receive their purchases while in the store. Rather, the purchases are shipped from a central warehouse direct to the consumer, simplifying the company's logistics, stock management, and processing.

While many traditional retail companies are irate about being used merely as local "fitting rooms" for customers who later make their purchases online, Bonobos uses this very effect to define its business model. Its retail spaces literally are nothing but fitting rooms, with customer fulfillment managed centrally, as with nearly all online companies. Bonobos' customers thereby obtain the best of both worlds. They get the shoppertainment experience of visiting a retail location, along with the low price and efficient service provided by online retail. Companies like Bonobos clearly show how retail is changing in our society. Companies that try to fight this trend will likely find themselves increasingly marginalized, and their stores increasingly empty of customers.

Other companies are seeking differentiation by implementing entirely new business models. Leading this charge of new players is Groupon, the ecoupon giant. Launched in 2009 and creating a new model of leveraged group buying power, Groupon has become the fastest company to reach $1 billion in revenues in history, taking less than three years to achieve this goal (See Figure 3.1)[6] Tellingly, the more money Groupon brings in, the less money is available to retailers and traditional channels of retail discounts. As such, the better Groupon performs, the bigger the bite that it is taking out of traditional retailers' revenue pies.

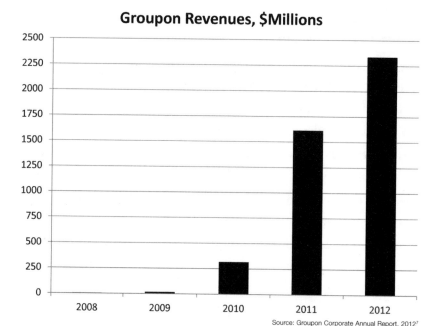

Source: Groupon Corporate Annual Report, 2012[7]

FIGURE 3.1. Groupon Revenues, 2008–2012

While Groupon's stock performance has been less than stellar, it's hard to argue with the success of its business model, in which Groupon identifies vendors who are willing to give significant discounts to buyers who combine their demand for products or services into a packaged deal. Retailers that create a Groupon deal give up some profit on each transaction that they sponsor (sometimes a significant percent of their profit) in return for selling to a larger group of customers. The total profit dollars that retailers receive is greater, but the profitability per transaction is significantly eroded. Add to this the fees that Groupon charges, and retailers are seeing a further loss of profitability.

The downside to Groupon is that its business model doesn't create value. Rather, it shifts value from retailers to customers. In the process, the company takes a cut for itself. Groupon might argue that through the deals that it arranges retailers receive more customers than they would without the group discount(s), thereby increasing the total market that a given retailer gets to serve. There may be some truth to this assertion. However it doesn't take away from the fact that Groupon is generating billions of dollars of revenue through transaction fees. These revenues could have been profit to the retailers who are using Groupon. Thus, the Groupon model is arguably accelerating the death of retail in today's marketplace.

Given the success of the Groupon business model, it was almost inevitable that others would develop further variations. One of the most recent and potentially successful variations is U-Deals, founded by the startup company Loopt. U-Deals follows a reverse-Groupon model. Rather than retailers creating packaged deals that they then sell to groups of customers, U-Deals collects groups of customers with a common need or want and aggregates their demand. U-Deals then offers the deal to the targeted vendor who can accept or reject it. U-Deals are necessarily location-specific, as the groups of customers must select the individual retailer to which they want to make the offer.

I believe that this semireverse auction model will prove to be as successful as Groupon. It's easy. It yields positive results to all parties, and it's a natural combination of socialfication and contextification, which we will discuss later. As with Groupon, the retailer gives up a degree of profitability per transaction in order to make more total profit dollars by selling to a group. Customers are happy because they are getting a better deal for a product or service that they wanted, and Loopt is happy because it gets a percentage of the transaction and lots of good customer data to analyze.

As smart as the U-Deals model is, it's likely that it will quickly be eclipsed by a true customer-driven reverse auction model, where groups of customers pull together their wants and needs and place their collective offer into a global marketplace. Rather than targeting a specific vendor, this model will allow any vendor to bid for the business, leading to much greater competition and potentially substantial savings for those customers who participate. And, of course, this model will further feed into the insipid decline of the retail sector, as its profits are continually eaten away by an ever-more knowledgeable and, therefore, more powerful base of customers.

When Opting Out Is Not an Option

What motivates retailers to participate in these markets? Why would any vendor willingly sacrifice profitability by signing up with Groupon, U-Deal, or any other customer aggregator? The answer is that early movers in these markets make gains at the expense of competitors who don't enter these markets. As mentioned, companies that provide deals on Groupon make less profit per customer, but the greater number of customers signing up for the deal allows the vendor to earn more total profit dollars. The participating vendor meets a larger proportion of the total market demand through heavy discounting. Those extra customers whom they receive do not, in turn, go to a competitor to have their needs met.

As such, there is a strong first-mover incentive for participating in these markets, particularly at the local level. For instance, if there are five pizza parlors in your hometown and you run the only one that provides Groupon-like deals, you might attract several more customers than you would without providing those deals. Given that you and your four competitors serve a relatively limited market, the more customers you gain for yourself, the fewer the customers that are left for your competitors. Assuming that even with the discounts you remain profitable on a per pizza basis, you will make more profit and be more successful than your four competitors. Indeed, you might be better placed to drive one or more of those competitors out of business, based upon your discounting activities.

Thus, the main motivation for companies to participate in these markets is simple: survival. For all companies, participation will necessitate systems that are integrated into these online markets. Such systems can identify customer-generated deals that appear to be relevant to the vendor and those that the vendor can respond to while remaining profitable on a deal-by-deal basis. This will require a degree of internal transparency that may be a significant challenge to many firms. How many retailers out there can determine their full-cycle profitability on every transaction? How many retailers are able to perform such an analysis in a predictive manner, thereby determining beforehand whether a transaction makes sense? And, given that most of these markets will operate on a reverse-auction model, how many retailers will be able to determine the price point at which they should stop bidding on each given auction that they are tracking in real time?

By 2020, chances are that such markets will capture a significant proportion, if not the majority, of most buyers' purchases. The value to the customer is too compelling, and there will be enough retailers participating to make the buying experience worthwhile to consumers. These markets will be yet another source of enormous amounts of data for companies to manage. Now, retailers will have to find relevant auctions to participate in, determine their own price constraints, determine if they can and should win a given auction, and then guarantee fulfillment if they do win. Further, each of these transactions will generate an enormous amount of customer data— data that will be invaluable to organizations that have established a fact-based operating model (described in Chapter 16).

In summary, ecommerce has grown beyond being an expansion of existing market share. Rather, it is the replacement of existing, traditional market share with cyber shares. As leading ecommerce innovators like Amazon drive the buying experience through their innovation, so they raise the bar for all companies that hope to remain competitive over the coming decade. Those who keep up or even leap ahead will enjoy tremendous growth in their market share and, as a result, enhanced profitability. They will gain this at the expense of companies that do not keep up with the state of the art in ecommerce and that choose instead to see their business continue to decline at an ever-accelerating rate.

Keeping up with ecommerce innovators means playing their game at least as well as they do. This means collecting, analyzing, and acting on vast quantities of customer data. And, mere analysis is not enough. Your business needs to acknowledge that customers are becoming ever more savvy, technology enabled, and fickle. Because of this, at a minimum your business needs to realign itself so that it can act upon customer demand in real time based on customers' needs from moment to moment. If you really want to keep up, you need to be able to predict customer needs and to fulfill them before anyone else does.

All of this means lots and lots of data. It's not enough to have it; you need to put it to work. We will explore the urgency of this message in the coming chapters, but be certain of this: If you think your company has a lot of information in its hands now, today's data volumes are perhaps less than one tenth of one percent of the data that your business will need to regularly use on a daily basis by 2020.

CHAPTER SUMMARY

1. By 2013, digital commerce had become mainstream, with $1.3 trillion transacted online.[8]

2. Given that customers are spending an ever-increasing proportion of their time online, companies that are focused on digital commerce will see their structural advantages over traditional companies continue to grow.

3. In the online world, your competition is not just those companies that provide the same products or services as your business. Rather, online, you compete for the attention of consumers with whichever company provides the best customer experience. As such, you compete with, and are likely falling far behind, companies such as Amazon.com, eBay, Target, and Groupon. Set your expectations of your own presence online according to these benchmarks, and try your best to catch up.

4

online entertainment
millions of channels, billions of actors

FROM STONE TABLETS to the Gutenberg printing press, from radio to television, every new communication technology created by humanity has led to dramatic social and cultural upheaval, transforming governments, altering expectations and cultural norms, and shifting power from one segment of the population to another. Interestingly, each of these major shifts has arrived in ever-shortening cycles, and their impacts on society have increased in both speed of adoption and rate of change in global culture.

With the adoption of the Internet, digital communication and digital entertainment have rocketed across the world, dramatically changing how the world's population communicates and entertains itself. As people spend more and more time online, the shift in their attention is causing dramatic changes in older media channels, such as print, music, television, and movies. While some of these traditional players will survive, or even thrive, in the digital age, most will fade away into irrelevancy. The difference between winners and losers may likely come down to whether a given player in the media and entertainment space can focus upon its message, rather than its medium and, as a result, stay engaged with its audience regardless of how those consumers chose to engage with the world.

YouTube: The 800-Pound Gorilla of Entertainment

When it was initially released to the world in 2005, YouTube was intended to fulfill a need for the sharing of personal videos on the Internet. At its introduction, few people beyond the company's founders believed that YouTube could ever be financially viable. Many Internet analysts believed that YouTube could never recover the cost of storage for all of the video files through advertising revenue; the business case simply didn't make sense to most people. And yet, YouTube was quickly gobbled up by Google, which immediately took to expanding the scale and scope of the service and leveraging the knowledge gained from being the largest search company on the web.

Flash forward seven years and YouTube had become the ultimate Internet video repository and is the third most visited website on the Internet.[1] In 2011, YouTube was accessed one trillion times,[2] and people watched a total of 35 billion hours of YouTube videos.[3] By 2013, if you weren't visiting YouTube at least once a week, you were part of a rapidly shrinking minority. On YouTube, visitors can see both highly polished videos created by professionals and the most rudimentary videos created by rank amateurs. Critically, every hour that users spend on YouTube is an hour they're not spending doing something else, like sharing time with family, working, watching TV, listening to the radio, or reading a newspaper.

As these numbers suggest, other forms of media are in serious trouble. For example, the 2012 finals on *American Idol*, then one of network TV's most popular shows, attracted 23 million one-time viewers for its most-anticipated, final episode,[4] making this one of the most-watched TV shows in recent history. Alternatively, *Annoying Orange*, a simple animated series on YouTube, attracted over 50 million views every month.[5] Hence, an unadvertised, unsponsored, home-made video series on YouTube is able to command double the audience per month than the most popular network television show. *Annoying Orange* gained so much attention and popularity that it was picked up by the traditional television Cartoon Network and became a regularly scheduled program.

This migration of artists from traditional channels to online channels is a natural consequence of three different market forces. First is the nearly five billion people with access to the Internet. Second, a large number, perhaps in the millions, of talented people have something to say to those five billion. And then third, the almost complete absence of start-up costs involved in putting content online. By 2013 there were over half a billion smart phones on the planet,[6] and most of them are able to shoot relatively high-quality video.

These days, if someone has something to say to the world, that person needs only to shoot a short video on a smartphone and then download the video to a YouTube account. Cable and satellite TV providers like to brag that they provide thousands of channels of programming. Yet, this pales to insignificance in light of the billions of hours of material that is now available online. Certainly, much of this material is low quality drivel, but the vast majority of people are absolutely hooked on these videos. Unfortunately, this is a direct re-flection of what the market for entertainment demands, and there will always be a portion of the population that favors "toilet humor." However, as more and more people spend more and more of their time on YouTube, there will be an ever-growing market pull for quality content. This transition may already be seen, particularly in videos that are now being sponsored by corporate advertisers.

Other forms of traditional media are experiencing serious decline. For instance, revenues from the sale of music on physical media (CDs, tapes, etc.) have been declining at over eight percent per year since 1999.[7] At the same time, digital record sales have been grow-ing at seven percent year after year.[8] Hence, while total sales of music are holding steady, sales of physical "records" are plummet-ing. We are fast approaching the end of the line for music retailers and, potentially, for traditional music distributors and record labels as well. Indeed, it is entirely likely that the CD will soon be obso-lete, going the way of the cassette, record, and eight-track tape.

In some ways, this is a boon for consumers . . . no more CDs or tapes or records taking up shelf space. But who hasn't lost or mis-placed digital files on a computer? How are you going to maintain all your music, movies, videos, and pictures across the 2.7 digital devices that the average American adult currently owns?[9] As much as the music and movie industries have fought the move to cloud-based entertainment solutions, platforms such as iTunes, Rhapsody, Amazon Prime, and Netflix have captured substantial market share in the entertainment industry. Traditional media companies are los-ing their market power to these virtual distribution channels, and they are not likely to be able to stop the migration of customers to virtual platforms for all forms of entertainment.

Nearly all other traditional media outlets are also in steep decline. For example, newspapers, once an extremely successful, extremely profitable business, have seen their advertising revenues drop by over 50 percent in the last five years.[10] Across the board, traditional media is finding an ever-increasing percentage of their audiences' time and attention being tied to digital media and, naturally, advertising revenues follow the eyeballs of the consumer.

Online Gaming and Immersive Entertainment

A further example of online entertainment that has become mainstream is gaming. While gamers used to be the butt of jokes about geeks without social lives, more and more people are signing up and logging into games for entertainment; particularly online game environments such as World of Warcraft, World of Tanks, Fly Aces High, and SimCity. These games provide immersive, virtual reality experiences to thousands of users simultaneously. Players can assume alternate identities, live alternate lives, and enjoy virtual experiences that might not otherwise be available to them. Indeed, some people find the experiences offered by these services to be so compelling that they become hooked. There are many reports of gamers becoming so obsessed by their virtual lives that their real lives begin to suffer. Results can be divorce, job loss, bankruptcy, and other life crises.

An extreme example of this phenomenon occurred in 2010 in South Korea. The parents of an infant became so hooked on an online game where they were raising a virtual baby that they actually allowed their real-world baby to die of malnutrition. They were subsequently charged with negligent manslaughter and were sentenced to five-year terms in prison.

Online gaming has become so popular that it is expected to grow from $16 billion in revenues in 2010 to approximately $30 billion by 2016, thereby almost doubling in six years.[11] To put this in perspective, in 2010 box office receipts from movies were worth $31.8 billion globally.[12] At this rate, online gaming should be a bigger business than Hollywood (and Bollywood) by around 2016.

The result of this surge in popularity of online gaming is the creation of new markets and new market opportunities. For example, in the online game World of Warcraft, players search through a virtual landscape and perform virtual tasks to collect virtual currency: gold pieces. Within the game, these gold pieces can be used to purchase virtual weapons, equipment, food, and other items, just like real currency in the real world. Typically, it takes quite a bit of game playing time to accumulate sufficient gold pieces to buy something useful. And, just like in the real world, the really cool stuff worth acquiring in World of Warcraft is particularly expensive in terms of gold pieces.

So, here you have millions of people spending a great deal of time playing a game to acquire cool stuff they want to possess. Does that sound like a business opportunity to you? It certainly did to many entrepreneurs in North Korea, China, and India, who started businesses in which they pay employees to play these online games for hours and hours every day. As these people play, they accumulate more and more virtual gold pieces, which they then put up for sale to other players in the real world. Effectively, these companies have formed an industry of game-playing outsourcing, where people can purchase virtual gold pieces in real-world marketplaces, such as eBay.

This business, known as gold farming, is no joke. In 2011, gold farming was estimated to be a $4 billion industry,[13] employing nearly a million people in countries like China and North Korea. What is remarkable is not that this business exists, but that game players take their game playing so seriously that they would spend $4 billion in real dollars to buy material trappings in a virtual world.

The take-away from these examples is that digital entertainment has experienced dramatic growth since the 1990s, so much so that traditional entertainment channels are suffering badly. There is every reason to expect this trend to continue, as more and more people are connected to the Internet every moment of every day. Mobile consumption of digital media, such as videos, has been growing at more than 70 percent year over year and is accelerating.[14] As such, more and more advertising dollars will flow into digital channels, and traditional media will continue to see dramatic declines in their business fortunes.

The Audience Is the Actor

One theme that is evident from the explosive growth of YouTube is that consumers want to play a more proactive role in their entertainment. Indeed, a large proportion of the content on YouTube is end-user created and represents millions of people searching for their own 15 minutes of fame. All of this content generation shows that consumers are looking to burn off a great deal of creative energy and are willing to invest a good deal of time and effort to get noticed.

As mentioned in Chapter 1, the recent release of smart glasses will almost certainly make YouTube even more popular to data consumers and an even larger repository of information. Smart glasses will allow people to readily record and post every aspect of their days, no matter how rudimentary the activity. And all evidence of YouTube use suggests that people will do exactly that: post hour after hour of video of their daily comings and goings.

The amount of data that will result from all of this recording is staggering to consider. If Google Glass is moderately successful, then it's a safe guess that by 2020, 100 million glasses will have been sold. If each user records only one hour of HD video every day, then they will collectively generate about 200 exabytes of data every year . . . just from Google Glass. That's a fifth of a zettabyte, which you'll recall from the introduction is a whole lot of data. So this one activity on this one platform, used sparingly, could itself increase the total size of global information traffic by twenty percent or more.

This likelihood is a remarkable understatement of how much data these tools will generate, and the idiom of always-on, always-connected that started with smart phones will reach a new plateau of data generation with the widespread adoption of smart glasses.

Smart glasses will be compelling to end users because they make each of us an actor in our own play. It plays on our egos and our need to feel that what we have to say is truly interesting. YouTube enabled people to feel special by allowing them 15 minutes of fame. In the coming age of smart glasses, everyone will want to feel this special every minute of every day. The opportunities for abuse of this capability are staggering. Similarly, companies that figure out how to connect with customers through their smart glasses experiences will reap rich rewards from the actors with whom they engage.

Without question, all of these changes to online entertainment are driving dramatic growth in the amount of information that is at the disposal of users. For entertainment companies, this means that they must create and freely distribute greater quantities of high-value content in order to remain relevant to their audiences. These companies must each become omnichannel distributors, pushing content through their traditional channels, as well as through online channels like YouTube. They must establish and maintain customer engagement with Facebook and Twitter, they need to release mobile apps that enrich their customers' entertainment experience, and they must find additional methods to allow audiences to actually participate in the entertainment experience, rather than passively receive it. This is a major change for these companies, and one that is not inexpensive. Many of these companies are spending tens or hundreds of millions of dollars on new facilities simply to store and maintain their vast libraries of digital content. That this need for an omnichannel presence comes at a time when their traditional revenue streams are failing puts these entertainment giants in a difficult position.

Indeed, these changes in consumer entertainment impact all companies because they are driving new expectations in the end-user community. While your products or services may not compete in the entertainment industry, you're still competing for your customers' attention. Those mechanisms that are most effective in creating customer engagement in ANY industry will quickly become the minimum standard that must be followed by EVERY industry that seeks to effectively market to consumers. As such, companies must broaden their view of their competition; it is more than just other companies in your industry, as the constraint that all companies are working against is the limited attention span of their customers.

CHAPTER SUMMARY

1. Online entertainment channels such as YouTube and online gaming sites are capturing an ever-growing proportion of consumers' free time.

2. Traditional media channels are in steep decline, and their remaining audience is growing more fickle, more impatient, and increasingly less relevant as a target market.

3. As mobility and social media continue to grow, marketers' ability to target individual consumers with customized mar-

keting messages will make mass-market advertising less effective and less relevant. This will further hurt the revenue streams of traditional media channels.

4. Online channels such as YouTube allow the audience to actually participate in the media experience. Customers will grow to expect such interactivity in their entertainment experiences, even when such engagement starts to look like work for the participant.

5. Audience interactivity will evolve from being a novelty to being an expectation, leading to new models of information consumption and creation. These media channels drive data growth in two primary ways. First, in the actual generation of the content, which is increasingly taking the form of high-definition video. The second is analyzing the consumption of all of this data, again to develop insights into end-user behavior, preferences, and connections, with the end goal of monetizing this information through targeted advertising.

5

cloud computing
the death of dedicated infrastructure

IF YOU ARE a business or technology professional in the 2010s, you have almost certainly heard about cloud computing. It seems that rarely a day goes by without your coming across some mention of the cloud in mainstream media and advertising. You probably use cloud services, such as iCloud, Dropbox, and Carbonite, and you're probably leveraging cloud technology in some way with nearly all of the companies that you interact with every day. Today, cloud computing may be the most hyped innovation in the global business environment. It's an example of the extreme commoditization of services and infrastructure that global markets are undergoing. (Commoditization is the almost complete lack of differentiation of a good or service.) However, information processing power is not the only area where this phenomenon is taking place.

Rather, ALL aspects of the business value chain are being reengineered. As a result, businesses that leverage outsourced services and infrastructure stand to become vastly more efficient and much faster in responding to changing customer demands. They are also much more efficient and effective at investing their funds in growth opportunities, as they can focus these funds on aspects of their business that provide differentiation. As discussed in Chapter 3, companies are being driven to focus upon either maximizing efficiency or maximizing perceived value to the customer. The commoditization that is taking place across all industries is a direct response to this trend.

Examples of this trend toward commoditization abound, from infrastructures, such as computing and networking, through common business processes, such as human resources, accounting, customer relationship management (CRM), and logistics. Indeed, the trend in most business processes is one of polarization. If a given business process does not differentiate your business, it should be outsourced and geared toward minimum cost and either maximum efficiency or maximum flexibility. This trend has led to the multitrillion dollar outsourcing industry, which continues to grow at double-digit rates every year.

Interestingly, this trend is highly dependent on the maturation of information technology, and the Internet in particular. By making the data of business processes instantly available, companies are able to outsource them and still maintain a degree of control over those processes. Indeed, such oversight is critical, as business executives are still held accountable for those business processes that they have outsourced.

The Utility Imperative: Why the World Is Moving to the Cloud

In some ways, the cloud computing business initially developed almost as an afterthought. Large-scale consumers of computing power recognized that they were able to achieve dramatic economies of scale by purchasing and building computing capacity. The key players in this market are Amazon, Google, and Microsoft, companies that have historically bought very large quantities of computing capacity to run their core businesses. It didn't take a financial genius to recognize that the purchasing power that these companies had would allow them to build excess computing capacity that they could then resell to others who might need it.

As is frequently the case with such innovations, these huge companies didn't invent cloud computing as a business, but they certainly legitimized it in the eyes of consumers. Leveraging their buying power (these three companies buy 20 percent of all of the world's server production every year[1]), and their focus on advanced computing (with Google and Amazon being particularly advanced users of "Big Data" analytics) has allowed them to build cloud services that meet challenging customer needs at significant cost savings.

Two primary drivers are behind corporate adoption of cloud computing. First, cloud computing dramatically improves IT resource utilization, thereby significantly reducing operating costs. An analysis by Manchester University in 2013 estimated that companies that embraced cloud computing reduced their IT costs by an average of 26 percent.[2] Given that the ongoing, accelerating growth of information will continue to drive increases in IT demands, this kind of reduction in operating costs is too great to ignore.

The second key driver in the adoption of cloud computing is that most cloud solutions provide a great deal of operational flexibility. If your organization suddenly requires more computing capacity, you simply sign up for more from your cloud provider. The cloud services provided by major vendors, such as Amazon and Microsoft, are supported by simply enormous infrastructures. As a result, they have plenty of excess capacity to go around. So customers of their cloud solutions could subscribe for hundreds or even thousands of more servers worth of computing capacity without having to worry about the provider's ability to meet the increased demand.

An interesting side effect of cloud services is that, for many customers, using clouds actually enhances the security and availability of their data. By 2010, the demand for experienced information security experts already far outstripped the supply. Most companies have such people on staff, but they might not be the best trained or most qualified people in the labor market. For cloud service providers, security is so critical to their business success that they are willing to invest heavily in the best security people, processes, and technology. Because of this, most cloud providers have far more effective information security infrastructures than even the biggest corporations. If you become a customer of one of these service providers, you have access to these security investments with the added benefit of a whole team of people whose sole job is to ensure that your data remains safe.

As a result, whether you are a commodity-based business seeking cost efficiency or a value-based business seeking maximum flexibility, cloud computing can provide significant support for your core operating model, while enhancing the security of your business information. This is what is leading to widespread adoption of cloud computing, and that same study by Manchester University found that 62 percent of American companies surveyed had adopted cloud computing in their business operations.[3]

Cloud and Competition: The End of Barriers to Entry

An interesting side effect of the growth of cloud is that it is feeding a whole new generation of startup companies. A generation ago, Internet startup companies were required to secure a couple of rounds of early venture funding to capitalize their business model. They used this seed money to purchase computing power, connectivity, and data capacity to launch their businesses. With a couple of millions of dollars, a startup could initially launch its business and see whether or not it would succeed in the market.

In today's world of cloud providers, this model is completely outdated. Now, when a startup has a new idea for an online business, the first thing is to buy a small amount of capacity with a cloud provider. The owners then launch and operate the business for a while to see if it will be successful and profitable. The capital required to reach this level of business maturity is measured in thousands of dollars, rather than millions. As a result, unlike 10 or 20 years ago, today's venture capitalists are extremely hesitant to fund a startup until after it has proven its model. Cloud computing facilitates this approach to investing.

Interestingly, cloud computing is so efficient for smaller companies that many don't need to secure additional funding to grow. Alternatively, those funds they do secure can be spent on marketing and demand generation, rather than on infrastructure. Since cloud computing is typically pay as you go and pay for what you use, a new business can easily scale up at the same rate as its revenue growth, no more and no less.

A further benefit of cloud solutions is that the scale up or scale out of services can occur almost instantaneously. If you need more computing power or more storage space, you click through a few web screens and the necessary capacity is instantly provisioned for your use. Smart companies use this on-demand capacity to handle any changes that might occur in their business volume from launching a new product or service, releasing a new promotion, or dealing with seasonal variation on demand. Hence, cloud services provide tremendous flexibility, frequently with a price advantage.

Such flexibility not only supports structural growth, but it also can help to handle seasonal variations in a company's business. Many companies, particularly in retail, see their business volumes expand greatly during the late Fall and early Winter holiday season. Indeed, many traditional retailers count on increased sales during the holidays to make their business profitable for the entire year. This increased volume of business necessarily increases the demand for computing capacity in their business systems. With cloud computing, these companies can subscribe to more computing capacity during those times that demand picks up and then dial back their subscription to cloud services once the peak demand has passed. This example shows how even a commodity-focused business can improve its efficiency by leveraging the flexibility of cloud computing.

Climbing the Value Chain: Expansion of the Cloud Paradigm

Over the past decade, cloud infrastructure services have grown to become a powerful force in the business world. At the same time, business process outsourcing has grown ever more commonplace in the market, as globalization and process standardization have made it easier and easier for companies to have common business processes outsourced to third parties that specialize in performing these processes with great efficiency.

Given the prevalence of outsourcing in the business world, it seems natural that more and more business processes and capabilities will follow the cloud paradigm. Rather than mere Infrastructure as a Service (IaaS), where someone else provides you with computing power and information storage, more and more companies will provide Platforms as a Service (PaaS), where entire business systems, such as ERP, SCM, or ECM, will be available as turnkey, online solutions. Such solutions exist today from companies like Workday, Salesforce.com, and Saperion. Further, even Microsoft has embraced this change and is providing the entire Office suite of software tools in a Software as a Service (SaaS) model. The evolution is clearly pointing toward larger and larger pieces of your business operations being delivered by third party suppliers.

What will follow PaaS and SaaS is what I'll call Outcomes as a Service (OaaS). Here, a business can subscribe to an outsourced service that is designed to produce a predictable business outcome. If a company is trying to hire a new employee, an OaaS service would provide a new, qualified employee as its outcome. If a company is trying to secure new customers in a new market, the identification of those new customers would be the outcome of an OaaS service that focuses on market generation.

OaaS will grow over the next decade as a result of the collision of a few different market dynamics. First will be the real-time availability of business data in standardized formats. For a company to take advantage of an OaaS provider, it must have a robust information infrastructure. The business must have a firm understanding of its internal business processes, so that it can integrate these with the processes and data used by the OaaS providers. This has been an ongoing goal of most companies over the last thirty to forty years. Recently, most companies are reaching the point where they can outsource key business processes while maintaining a degree of control through the data that they create and manipulate.

The business processes and services that will fall into the cloud delivery model will continue to expand and move up the business value chain. While traditionally simple business processes, such as recruiting, payroll, and shipping, have been commoditized and out-sourced for years, more advanced business services are now being simplified, aggregated, and made outsourceable. Recently, I've noticed several new services being advertised on television, including LegalZoom for legal services, 1800Accountant for accounting services, and so on. While these OaaS providers are initially targeting the small and medium business market, it is inevitable that these business services will continue to be commoditized and subsequently delivered in a cloud-like model to ever larger organizations. Larger organizations have more business and more revenue to bring to these OaaS providers, and those same large businesses are constantly looking for ways to improve their bottom lines.

As more and more business processes standardize through the wave of OaaS migration, a new trend will begin to evolve: that of Everything as a Service (EaaS). In an EaaS world, a company will be able to look at every single business process that it requires to operate and will be able to determine which steps of each process add value and differentiate the company's products or services, as well as which ones don't. Speed, efficiency, and cost effectiveness will necessitate that nonvalue-added processes be outsourced to an OaaS provider as much as possible. EaaS will come into play when some companies start aggregating other OaaS providers to create one-stop shops for business process outsourcing. Through an EaaS provider, a company could literally start with a business plan and be up and running in a matter of weeks or days with fully formed, robust business processes that can immediately support the business.

Cloud computing is currently passing through its marketing hype cycle and is rapidly become a standard business model in a wide range of industries. There are, and will remain, some concerns surrounding the use of cloud computing, including information security and maintaining control over sensitive information. However, these concerns will be addressed by cloud service providers as their offerings mature and as market acceptance of cloud computing as a normal operating paradigm continues. And, as mentioned at the beginning of this chapter, many cloud providers actually have stronger, more advanced, and more vigilant information security systems than the largest of the Fortune 500 companies. The operational efficiency and flexibility provided by cloud computing are so compelling that this approach to resource utilization will almost certainly expand to encompass all aspects of how businesses operate. As such, in the near future, we may find that nearly every business outcome may be achieved through the use of a third party's virtualized resources and, as a result, entire virtual industries may arise with almost no capital investment. This may have profound impacts on market competition and the drive toward efficiency or innovation by larger companies, as barriers to market entry literally disappear into a number of clouds.

CHAPTER SUMMARY

1. Cloud computing is providing dramatic improvements in operational efficiency and flexibility for those companies that have adopted this approach to service delivery. Many companies are seeing their computing costs drop by thirty percent or more when they move to the cloud.

2. Cloud computing is expected to be a trillion dollar business by 2015.[4]

3. More and more services will become virtualized in the future. Clouds will grow beyond mere infrastructure and will begin to migrate into markets higher up in the corporate value chain. This trend will rapidly lead to Everything as a

Service (EaaS) marketplaces, where nearly any business outcome can be purchased by an outside provider.

4. Successful companies will be those that rapidly and comprehensively buy into this EaaS business approach, thereby minimizing operating costs and maximizing business flexibility.

5. You are likely outsourcing at least some of your business processes today. In the future, look to start breaking down processes into incremental outcomes, and then seek outsourcers that can provide these incremental outcomes through cloud-based outcome markets.

6

"big data"
learning from the flood

AS WITH THE other social and business trends already discussed, Big Data is an area of business that has received tremendous hype over the last several years. Most business executives have heard this term in recent times, and many of those same executives wonder what exactly "Big Data" is and "How do I get some in my company." As is typically the case with new business concepts, Big Data is surrounded by mystery and treated as if it were a panacea to all of a company's ills. While there may be some truth to this, the reality of Big Data is far less mysterious and far more practical than many industry pundits make it out to be. Let's take a quick dive into the world of Big Data so that you can see its underpinnings and potential value to your business.

The Data Revolution: From Storage to Knowledge

At its most basic, Big Data is nothing more than the application of statistical analysis to very large quantities of information. There are more sophisticated forms of Big Data, where advanced technology is used to determine if groups of data have a "tone" or contain "sentiment," and there are still further technologies that blend structured data, such as business records, with unstructured data, such as email. The goal is finding new insights into user behavior. Fundamentally, Big Data is the application of mathematical, statistical, and scientific principles to the interpretation of extremely large amounts of data.

What constitutes a large amount of data? In 2012, every 60 seconds there were over 200 million emails sent in the United States, Twitter received over 100,000 tweets, and YouTube received over 48 hours of new video. As of 2013, Facebook was collecting over 500 terabytes of user data every day,[1] which is the equivalent of over 500 very large computer hard drives. This data is constantly cross-referenced with all of the previous data Facebook has collected, which by now represents a colossal database of our personal preferences, opinions, and habits. When this data is analyzed by statisticians, psychologists, marketers, and scientists, the degree to which Facebook and *its* customers (other companies) understand you and your preferences is nothing short of staggering!

Big Data is receiving enormous amounts of press these days, and yet there's a complete lack of consensus on what exactly constitutes "Big Data." After all, haven't companies analyzed their data for decades? Haven't they mined their existing data to gain new insights into how to improve operations, or how to serve customers better, or how to reduce defects?

Back in the 1980s I worked for General Electric as an engineering intern. Most of my time on that eight-month assignment was spent analyzing and trying to learn from defective data from one of its computer production lines. Thus, I'm quite certain that data analysis is nothing new. In fact, any company that hasn't been mining its existing *transactional* data for insights by this time has probably already gone out of business. So the first part of our definition of "Big Data" is defining what it is not; "Big Data" is not the analysis of corporate structured, transactional data . . . the sort of stuff that is stored in ERP, CRM, SCM, and other traditional corporate systems.

So, then, is "Big Data" the process of analyzing unstructured, collaborative systems such as email, collaboration platforms like SharePoint, or corporate social platforms like Jive? Again, the answer is "no." Unstructured data generally doesn't lend itself to statistical analysis; fifty thousand business emails might contain not a scratch of corporate intelligence, and yet one particular email or web post might be worth millions to a company if it can be found and acted upon. Unstructured data is more easily mined using search tools or through social processes, the gamification that we will address later.

So, we have just defined two things that "Big Data" is not. So, what is it? Expanding on the definition offered at the beginning of this chapter, Big Data really consists of two things. First, it is the joint analysis of structured and unstructured data from within a company. Second, it is the joint analysis of internal data sources and external data sources, both structured and unstructured, again to find new insights. Naturally, both of these types of analysis have an element of "bigness" to them, implying that the sources of data are measured in terabytes, if not petabytes or even exabytes. Let's explore these two variations on Big Data, so that I can defend this definition to you.

In my first definition of Big Data, I have companies combining two dissimilar forms of data and analyzing the result for new insights. Structured and unstructured data sets are like oil and water; they don't play nicely with each other, and they don't lend themselves to rigorous statistical analysis. For instance, your financial system might have a bunch of transactional data on how many widgets you've sold to customer X over the years. Similarly, your corporate email system might have thousands of emails that mention Customer X for some reason or another; therefore, it represents an unstructured source of data about customer X. A Big Data scientist would combine the structured transactional data with all emails that mention customer X over a similar time frame to see if there are correlations between what customer X has bought over the years and the information in the emails.

This sort of analysis constitutes "Big Data" for a few reasons. First, the datasets are probably quite large. It's not uncommon for large companies to have email repositories and transactional databases in the petabyte range, with millions or even billions of records to sort through (recall the sales volumes of Walmart, for example). Second, this sort of analysis falls under Big Data because it requires sophisticated analysis tools, such as natural language search or semantic search to work effectively. These are the same techniques and tools used for the other form of Big Data; they're just used against internal data sets exclusively. Finally, I qualify this sort of analysis as "Big Data" because most companies have never mined the combination of structured and unstructured internal data before. As such, those companies that begin this process stand to discover dramatic insights into their operations, their customers, their employees, and the markets that they serve; insights that they would not readily gain by any other means. As such, this sort of joint analysis of internal, structured, and unstructured data represents "Big Data," if only because it can generate big impacts for the business.

Companies that tap into this first class of "Big Data" analysis can then effectively take advantage of the second class, which is combining internal data sources, both structured and unstructured, with external data sources. Those external sources may also be either structured or unstructured, or both, depending on the questions being asked. Again, part of the key value of these analyses is that they haven't been done before; in fact, they may not have even been possible prior to the last four or five years.

These analyses can take the "Big" of "Big Data" to a whole new level of enormous. Think of the 600 terabytes of unstructured data that Facebook collects every day from its users or the multipetabytes of structured data stored by each of the departments of any state or national government or by industry organizations. Tapping into these sources can unlock untold riches in key insights about your business. But given the scale and scope of these data sources, you're better off learning the ropes of "Big Data" analysis by initially focusing on your own data, than tapping into the Niagara Falls of external sources that are available.

A simple example might add some clarity here. Let's pretend that you're the owner of a soda vending machine company, with two hundred vending machines located throughout your local county. You have several dozen drivers who travel on regularly scheduled routes to check and ensure periodically that each vending machine doesn't run out of soda. Over time, your drivers have noticed a great deal of variability regarding which soda machines sell a lot of their inventory and which sell very little. You have many years worth of data on these variations in inventory, but could never seem to find any logical patterns to explain why one machine might go weeks without using up its inventory and then suddenly become empty over the course of a day or two.

If we combine some nontraditional data with that at our business' disposal, we may start to find some interesting trends that will help us understand the variations in demand that our data show. For instance, if we were to combine our sales data with that of the local weather around each vending machine, we may find that temperature, humidity, and precipitation all have an impact on soda sales. It would stand to reason that when it is hot and humid, cold drink sales increase, but our analysis could both validate and quantify this belief.

Further, let's say that most of our vending machines are in public locations near shopping malls, schools, and public transportation hubs. If we were to join our sales data with data related to special events in each of these locations, we may again find some strong correlations. For instance, we may find that machines located near high schools rapidly sell out over weekends when there is a football game at the school. Or, when the local mall has a big promotional event like a music show, our machines at that store similarly run out of stock very quickly.

By combining our traditional datasets with nontraditional data sets, we can start to uncover underlying findings in the collective data sets that are not obvious when looking at them separately. These nontraditional data sets are typically very large, hence the term "Big Data," and they typically capture relevant external factors that our traditional data collection lacks. This, then, is the value of Big Data analysis. It expands the volume and variety of data at our disposal, such that our analyses can seek out and find new intelligence that we otherwise would have missed.

Data Analysts: The Rock Stars of the Data Age

Back in the late 1990s, during the first Internet boom, computer programmers were in extremely short supply. There weren't a lot of people who knew the latest software languages, like Java, and every company needed people with those skills to establish themselves on the web. As a result, programmers could name their own price in the labor market. Most had four or five job offers to choose from at any one time, and most also received unheard of perks, such as leased

BMWs, pets at work, and catered lunches on the job. At the time, we referred to these people as Java rock stars, because they could literally ask for and get their every need met by their eager employers.

It's safe to say that most of these people had a hard time dealing with the subsequent Internet crash of 2000, when all of the perks, the stock options, and the income quickly disappeared. Suddenly, being a programmer no longer guaranteed a steady six-figure salary. This trend has continued into the present decade, as software has advanced and become easier to use, and more and more technical work is outsourced to overseas developers. For programmers, the bust cycle has far outlasted the boom cycle that preceded it.

We are entering the beginning of yet another boom cycle in skill sets, one that is driven off of the need for people who understand and can make sense of large quantities of data. Statistics and probabilities are the new in-demand languages, as more and more companies attempt to put their humungous piles of data to work.

One outcome of this data revolution is certain: the demand for people who are data literate will grow dramatically over the coming decade. In its study on Big Data released in May 2011, the strategy consulting firm McKinsey forecasted that there would be a shortage of at least 1.5 million people with this skill set by 2015.[2] Thus, there will be a dramatic shortage of people with these skills precisely at the time when their skills are in greatest demand. These people will command a significant premium for their skills for the foreseeable future; hire yours while you still can!

Making Data Pay: The Rising Role of Personalization and Customization

To understand the power of Big Data analytics, one need only look at retail powerhouses, such as Target. While other retailers are struggling merely to survive in the current competitive climate, Target is posting some stellar growth numbers, quarter after quarter. Indeed, Target's revenues grew from $44 billion in 2002 to nearly $70 billion in 2012, despite having to weather the Great Recession at the end of the first decade of the 2000s.[3] Target attributes part of this growth to its greater customer focus and better understanding of customer needs. This is business speak for having implemented data analytics to better meet the targeted needs of customers; pun intended.

A most notable example of Target's use of data analytics is the story of the teenage girl who started to receive coupons in the mail from Target. The coupons included deals on diapers, baby clothes, and car seats, the stuff that a typical expecting mother would be interested in buying. The girl's father found the mailing and was furious with Target for trying to encourage his daughter to get pregnant. He went down to his local Target store to complain to the store manager, who apologized profusely on the company's behalf. On a subsequent follow-up with the father, however, the manager was told that the girl was indeed pregnant and had been holding out on telling her father about it. He found it out first from Target!

This begs the question: How did Target know that the girl was pregnant? Through its customer analytics effort, Target had determined that if a customer purchased any combination of about twenty products, there was an excellent chance that she was pregnant. Some of these products were obvious, such as morning sickness pills. Others were less obvious, such as scent-free lotion, light blue or pink blankets, or multivitamins. When all of these purchases were taken together, Target could determine whether a customer was pregnant with remarkable accuracy. And then, the company could send those customers targeted marketing messages, coupons, and other deals in order to capture their business. This example was particularly relevant, given the tendency of expecting parents to have an expansive list of items to buy, and a strong motivation to spend their money on items they anticipate needing.

This example shows that through comprehensive data analysis, businesses can develop a new level of understanding about what drives customer behavior. This information can then be used to change both what and how they sell to their customers, potentially driving both revenue and profit growth for those customers who have been targeted. Quantitative analysis such as this is readily achievable today, and many of the most successful companies in the world are using such analysis as a core differentiator to their business.

CHAPTER SUMMARY

1. Through the 2010s, data analysis will become a key differentiator between successful companies and also-rans. Those companies that put their data to work to develop deep customer insights will create a lead over competitors that may quickly become insurmountable.

2. Market leaders, such as Amazon.com, Google, and eBay, have set the bar for customer expectations in personalized online experiences. Any company that wants to remain relevant to its customers must learn from these market leaders and do their best to keep up with the state of the art in creating a customer-centric, personalized experience online.

3. Business people at all levels must become data literate in the near future. Analytics will drive nearly all business decisions, particularly as the volume, velocity, and variety of data continues to accelerate.

part two

the impact on business

While much of the information in Part I may not be news to you, it was important to discuss why organizations are facing data crush before delving into what changes this crush is driving into the business environment. Part II reviews some of this impact and the trends that massive data volume is generating throughout our society.

As you review these trends, or "-ifications," it may become apparent that while the growth in data that we've experienced thus far this century has been impressive, we have only scratched the surface of data growth. Each of the trends discussed will naturally lead to accelerated data growth in a self-reinforcing, self-fulfilling manner. If there is one message that I hope to get across through this discussion it is this: If you want to remain relevant to your customers in the coming years, it is imperative that you embrace these trends and align your business strategies to the new world into which they are leading us.

7

contextification
responding to the market of one

CONTEXTIFICATION is the trend by which people will be addressed by others based upon their place in the world. This context is their "where" and "when" in Albert Einstein's space–time continuum. By this I mean that a person's place in space and time determines their context, and this context determines what information they may be interested in and what data they may be generating as a result. Context is the dominant determinant of what is of immediate interest to a data consumer and, as such, contextification will become the primary driving force behind how organizations engage with their target audiences.

The Importance of Where and When
Chapter 2 included an introduction to the concept of context services, in which mobile devices are given the ability to know when

and where they are in the world. These devices can then expose their users to information based upon these two factors. This process of making use of context services may be called *contextification*, a process through which companies will find a wide continuum of potential services to provide to their customers.

If you own a smartphone, you have certainly experienced early generations of contextification. If you launch a mapping app from your phone and location services have been enabled, the phone figures out where you are in the world (and when) and will display your location on the map inside of the app. If you then searched for something in the app, say "gas station," the app would find gas stations closest to your position and display them on the map. This is contextification, where your location in space and time become part of your search criteria.

Contextification has only been possible since the early 2000s, as it required mobile services companies to incorporate location information into their service architectures and then to expose this data to outside companies, such as app developers. As such, much of what is possible through contextification is yet to be realized. However, given the rapid expansion of smartphones and apps throughout the world, the demand for, and expectations of, contextification should see this realm of technical capabilities grow dramatically. And, as contextification takes off, these advanced services will increase the volume of data created by our civilization by a couple of additional orders of magnitude.

The impact that contextification has upon data crush cannot be understated. For each of us, our context in the world constantly changes. We may continually change our position by going to work, the store, or another city or country. Most of us change our position in the world pretty frequently throughout our day. On top if this physical movement is our movement through time. Adding this fourth dimension to our context truly leads to data crush, as every second of our lives provides a new and different context, where our wants and needs may change second by second.

For example, a fast-food chain that is trying to entice you to stop by one of its restaurants will find the "when" of your context as important as your "where." It wouldn't be terribly useful to send a nearby customer a coupon for a half-price breakfast sandwich at 2 PM (or perhaps it would be, for the right customer.). However, 2 PM might be a great time to send that customer a coupon for half off on a lunch meal.

So, by using these four contextual dimensions, three spacial dimensions plus time, we effectively create trillions of unique market opportunities. Unfortunately, this means that businesses must become aware of these trillions of opportunities, track them in real time, and act upon them in real time. This is data crush in action and is rapidly becoming the new normal for customer-oriented business.

Additionally, further dimensions may be incorporated into contextification that would further refine unique market opportunities. An example is local weather conditions. Smart phones are aware of their local weather either by datafeeds from the network or by measuring devices directly on the phone, such as a thermometer and barometer. What value does this add to a person's context? If a person is outside in 90-degree heat, you may want to send a coupon for an iced latté rather than a hot beverage. Conversely, if it is snowing at the customer's location, you may want to offer a deal on a hot chocolate.

Another set of dimensions that is rapidly gaining popularity is personal wellness data. Customers presently have access to a range of smart devices and apps that keep track of health-related data, such as blood pressure, body temperature, and distances covered each day. These datasets can feed ever-deepening contextification, giving companies a richer data set with which they can understand and sell to customers. Of course, these additional context dimensions dramatically increase the amount of data to be managed and analyzed, but we already know that this will be the new normal for businesses that wish to remain in business.

Another reason that contextification is driving massive data growth is how companies are responding to all of this context data. Each unique context that you might identify for your customers, and again there may be billions of them, defines a unique use case. For each of these use cases, there is an optimal offer of a product or service that you might provide. As such, if you are collecting enough data on customer context to define 10,000 unique use cases, you should strive to have a similar number of unique responses, or offers, to each of them.

For instance, if I need a limo at a particular cross street in Manhattan, I represent a unique market of one at that street at that instance. Knowing this is insufficient to make a transaction happen. It's not enough to know that a specific demand exists. You must also be able to respond to that market of one. Thus, a limo company not only needs to know that I need a limo right now at that location, it also must track where all of the company's limo's are at any moment so that it can send the closest limo to my location, thereby meeting my need. To monetize contextification, knowing your response is as important as knowing that the demand exists.

Ideally, I have at least as many unique responses to contextual use cases as I have use cases, as each use case has an optimal response. If I have only one response to each of 10,000 possible use cases that have been identified, there is no value in knowing all of that contextual detail. The outcome is that the resulting data crush comes not only from analyzing all of the data that is being generated by customers; it also comes from creating all of the unique responses that you will have to each of those use cases.

Meeting Customer Needs Before They Have Them

As anyone who has used mapping apps on their smartphone knows, contextification is just plain cool. Apps that know when and where I am, along with my preferences, and then present me with information or options based upon this data are very compelling to the user. With these apps, I can instantly find information that is immediately useful to me, regardless of what I may be looking for at that moment. Am I hungry right now? No problem, here are the closest 10 or 20 eateries. Do I need to put gas in my car? With a click I can find the five or six closest gas stations. Having trouble finding a parking space downtown? By early 2013, there are apps that help you find the closest open parking space.

Contextification is a game-changing social trend because it breaks down each of our days into thousands and thousands of individual chunks. Each chunk is one in which we can define our immediate needs and wants, thereby creating a unique, time- and space-boxed market. Each of these markets, necessarily markets of one, can be extremely well defined and thus readily targeted by companies. Because of the specificity, indeed uniqueness, of each of these markets, any company that can meet a customer's need at that precise moment creates much higher customer value. As a result, the company can earn significantly more of that customer's business than it otherwise might. By this process, contextification facilitates the creation of limitless new opportunities to identify, define, and then meet our wants and needs.

Meeting customers' in-context needs is just the beginning of contextification. As the technologies and data underpinning contextification grow, there will be an increasing ability to actually predict a user's future context. From this will grow the ability to predict future needs, thereby creating market "pull" rather than market "push." This shift will fundamentally change consumers' definition of good customer service. In the near future, being responsive to customers will be a ticket to market failure. Rather, being predictive of consumers' wants and needs will be expected. Keep in mind that this shift from responsive to predictive marketing relies on the real-time analysis of vast quantities of contextual data, and that this contextual data will continue to expand at alarming rates. As big as your present data management challenges may seem, they are trivial compared to how complex they will become over the coming decade.

To participate in this contextified world, users will necessarily have to sacrifice a degree of privacy. Indeed, the more privacy you're willing to give up, the greater the potential returns through contextification. As we're already seeing, some people flatly refuse to make this tradeoff. Others readily throw caution to the wind and dive head first into the context-enabled marketplace. This effect has some generational undertones, as younger users of mobile and social technologies appear to be dramatically less concerned about their privacy than older users. While we're likely to see these generational trends continue, there will be mounting pressure to "opt in" to the contextification wave because the benefits to the end user will be so compelling.

Trillions of Markets of One

As more and more companies begin to mine the huge amounts of data at their disposal, they are creating and supporting this new dynamic of mass customization in the consumer market. Frequent users of sites like Amazon.com, Google, and eBay will recognize this trend, as these sites actively profile each of their visitors and use the resulting information to sell more products to them, thereby becoming indispensable in meeting customer needs. In the process, these sites become customized to the user's preferences, present requests, and predicted future needs.

This customer-centric approach is leading to a new market paradigm: the Market of the Individual Consumer. Consumers now expect this degree of targeted experience from all their interactions with companies. Companies that succeed at this will realize dramatic growth and improved profitability. Conversely, companies that fail to deliver this customized experience will find themselves increasingly marginalized and pushed into commodity niches of product or service delivery. They will also see their profitability evaporate, as they fail to effectively respond to individual users' needs and expectations.

Interestingly, this focused targeting does not necessarily reduce the quantity of messages that consumers receive from vendors; rather, messages that are received will tend to be dramatically more relevant and will consume more of the customer's limited attention, further exacerbating the problem of information overload.

The market of the individual consumer is both enabled by and feeds the dramatic growth in customer data, so companies are now repositories of vast quantities of customer information and must actively mine and respond to this data in real time. This places tremendous demands on the companies' information resources. It will also drive significant changes in how successful companies operate.

With even further application of contextification, a company might know who my friends are in the city I am traveling to, what their availability is to meet with me while I'm in town, and the name of their favorite local restaurant. This information enables a marketing person to create a hypertargeted message to send to me during those thirty seconds he or she has my attention to get me to buy something. The likelihood that I will respond positively to the commercial (and hence, spend my money) goes up dramatically, since it meets my immediate, contextual need. The effectiveness of the marketing dollars spent by the sponsor through contextification grows dramatically.

It is this outcome efficiency that will drive vast amounts of marketing dollars into contextification over the coming decade. This will be particularly true in the mobile space, where contextification is most powerful because the end user is constantly moving through potential markets. Indeed, in 2012 mobile marketing spending increased by nearly 80 percent over 2011, and such growth rates are expected to accelerate over the coming years.[1]

You can also find similar contextification on YouTube, where in order to watch many popular videos you must first view a short commercial. The contextification here is superficial and fairly weak; it is based on the content of the video that you're trying to view. However, it is highly likely that over the next few years the commercialization of YouTube will grow dramatically, particularly as more and more users access YouTube via mobile devices. As contextualization becomes more possible, it will become more probable.

Microeconomies: Responding to the Microneeds of Micromarkets

One natural side effect of contextification will be the growth of microeconomies. Once it is possible to track every second of every customer's day, it will be possible to market to them only during those few seconds each day that my product or service would be of particular interest. As such, companies will be able to focus their marketing messages and dollars on just those few seconds each day when a particular customer is in the right context to be a probable customer, rather than merely a potential customer. Such targeted marketing is vastly more effective, dollar for dollar, than traditional mass-market advertising. Thus, contextified marketing, and thereby microeconomies, will become normal over the coming decade.

Microeconomies will become prevalent because of two trends: the cost of executing a transaction is rapidly approaching $0, and contextification is creating infinite opportunities for transactions to take place. If every incremental combination of customer time and place produces a potential opportunity for a customer purchase to occur and the cost of launching that potential transaction is vanishingly small (approach fractions of a penny per transaction), then these transaction are likely to occur and will occur in the trillions of events per day.

Examples of this trend already exist. Some banks now set up credit and debit cards so that each customer transaction is rounded up to the nearest dollar with the additional money added to the customer's savings account. So, if a customer spends $24.83 on gas, the transaction is automatically rounded up to $25 and the incremental $.17 is placed in his or her savings account. Or, I presently belong to a frequent-buyer club at a local grocery chain. As I spend more money, I earn discounts for purchasing gasoline at a station a block away. These vendors constantly sync their customer data in real time and create a cross-market synergy with their common customers.

There are other examples where customers earn products, services, or cash by spending their valuable time watching a targeted ad. For example, San Francisco Airport has Wi-Fi Internet access set up throughout its terminals which anyone can access. However, to connect to the Internet through this service, users must agree to watch a 30-second commercial. This is a microeconomy in action;

I give 30 seconds of my time and attention to receive a product or service that is valuable to me, 15 minutes of Internet access.

What is interesting is that these microeconomies are vastly more efficient and effective from the marketer's point of view. Marketers have a vast array of means to reach their customers, and they are always looking for the most cost-effective way to influence the market. The advantage of microeconomies is that their audiences can be deeply understood and hence finely targeted, allowing the marketing message to be honed to its greatest effect. But, nothing is free, so to leverage microeconomies, companies must collect, process, and act upon the torrent of data being created by contextification.

In the previous example of airport Internet access, companies pay for the service in return for my watching their commercial. What do marketers know about me when they create a commercial for me to watch? They know that I travel. They likely know what airline I am traveling with. They know that I use the Internet while I travel. With a greater application of contextification, they might know my travel plans, including my destination, my ground arrangements, and my car rental company. All of these can be used to target products and services that may be of interest to me.

It should be apparent that this trend will lead to a further explosion in data growth. Making a $50 purchase 10 cents at a time necessarily increases the number of transactions involved by a factor of 500. Yet, this sort of digital layaway will become commonplace over the next decade. If consumers are able to break down their attention span into individual seconds, they can then sell each of those seconds to the highest bidder among advertisers. Whatever value the customer receives from the marketers may be trivial on a per-transaction basis. But, aggregated over hours, days, and weeks, these micropayments will start to add up to real money and real value to the consumer. By adding the results of customer responses to this vast quantity of microcommercials to the databases currently used to model customer behavior, companies will be able to further refine their messaging and greatly increase the yield that they receive from their marketing dollars. Taken together, all of this means an enormous increase in the amount of data being generated, stored, and analyzed by these companies.

Contextification Maturity Model

The maturity model for contextification is shown in Figure 7.1. Such models are nothing new to the world of software; a similar maturity model was developed by Carnegie Mellon University in the 1990s that allowed organizations to determine the maturity of their internal software development processes. Here, I define a contextification maturity model with levels 0 through 5. These six levels define a sliding scale of complexity and capability in contextification.

Contextfication CMM

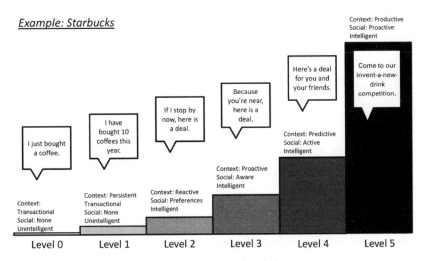

FIGURE 7.1. Contextification Maturity Model

At level 0, no contextification is present. At level 5, an organization has achieved highly advanced contextification. Each step in between represents an incremental increase in capability and complexity, and similarly each level implies a greater generation and use of information.

Proceeding to the contextification maturity model, Level 0 shows anonymous transactions like a customer purchasing something from you with cash. Such a transaction provides no context about that individual consumer or that particular transaction. As such, the seller has little to learn from the transaction, other than the fact that there happened to be at least one customer for the item that was purchased. You might know the time that the purchase took place and the price paid, but not by whom. Hence, these datapoints could not be assigned to a given customer and have little value against the infinite markets of one that contextification provides.

Level 1 contextification is where a customer may either pay for the transaction with a credit or debit card or use a frequent buyer card of some sort. This provides some context for that particular consumer, but it is generally after the fact. Once the transaction has taken place, the new transaction can be added to those made by that same consumer in the past, thereby generating a transactional history I can track. Thus, it is persistent. From Level 1, we can look at a customer's buying history and start to understand some of his or her behaviors and preferences. Here, at Level 1, we can first begin to apply sales information to particular consumers, and thereby begin to understand them.

At Level 2, we finally begin to be context aware. We know when and where a customer is in the world, and we are able to act on this information once we have it. Additionally, our understanding of the customer may be improving, and we can start to put his or her behaviors and preferences into context. The time and location data that becomes available with Level 2 contextification has been available for some time at retail locations. However, with mobility there are now millions of moments of context that can be leveraged for each and every customer. As such, Level 2 contextification can become vastly more powerful for achieving customer outreach and will also result in dramatically greater volumes of data to wade through.

With Level 3, we start to recognize patterns to a customer's context, which allows us to target the customer proactively. Because we have seen a customer act in a particular way in the past, we can expect similar activity in the future. This is using historical contextual information to predict, and verify, future contexts into which the customer might enter. Further, we can gain more context by starting to follow the customer on social media platforms. By adding this information and a more sophisticated model of preferences, a customer's perspective of us can begin to develop.

With Level 4 contextification maturity, we have enough of an understanding of a customer's behavior to merge predictive modeling with a user's social media data to create life events for the customer. We might know that a customer is traveling to Boston this week and that three friends will also be in town. Based on this, we'll invite the foursome to dinner at a Boston restaurant at a special discount.

At Level 5 contextification, we're actually using our knowledge of the customer to produce productive outcomes for both ourselves and for the customer. At this level, we're engaging with the customer in a way that puts that person to work for us, even as he or she continues to buy goods or services from us. Socially, we've developed a proactive relationship with the customer. We're anticipating future needs and actually changing those needs by using the influence we've earned by nurturing an ongoing relationship. Using the Boston trip example above, we'd advance that example to Level 5 contextification by having the participants post reviews, videos, and other content about their dinner experience on various websites and social platforms, thereby promoting our business.

Contextification Example: Starbucks Coffee

An example is worth a thousand words, so let's make up a hypothetical situation to illustrate what I've outlined above. Let's say that I like Starbucks coffee (as, indeed, I do). And, let's say that Starbucks is a forward-thinking company that recognizes the value of understanding its customers (as, indeed, it does) and, as a result, the company tries to get to know me better as a customer.

Skipping over maturity Levels 0 and 1, if Starbuck's contextification maturity is Level 2, then it knows about my past behavior. So, if I've bought coffee at Starbucks 15 times in the last year, the company knows that. It will also know what I ordered (a dark, venti blackeye), how I paid (assuming that I used a credit card or a frequent buyer card of some sort, Level 1 stuff), and where I made my purchases (Redlands Boulevard, also Level 1). From its Level 2 knowledge of me, the company knows that if I'm targeted with a generic coupon, there's some chance that I might stop by Starbucks more often.

Let's now assume that Starbucks has advanced to Level 3, meaning that it is aware of my context; it knows my when, my where, who I am, and my preferences. With this level of contextification, it would know WHEN I am driving past that Starbucks on Redlands Boulevard and, therefore, when the company should offer me an instant coupon I can use if I drop by in the next 15 minutes. With this knowledge and Starbuck's real-time response, I am far more likely to stop by at the moment I receive the message, thereby increasing the revenue that Starbucks is likely to receive from me. For most retailers, Level 3 represents a step up from the common practice of customer loyalty cards and can potentially be served by the new generation of apps that are being deployed on smartphones. These apps can feed contextual information to vendors, allowing them to model their customers' contextual behaviors.

Now let's advance to Level 4 contextification, in which Starbucks can *predict* my wants and needs, potentially before even I am aware of them. Once Starbucks can track my where and my when, it wouldn't be too hard for employees to figure out that I drive by the Redlands Boulevard store every workday between 7:30 and 8:00 AM. Knowing this, they could actually predict my future context and make me offers based upon this future context. If they know that I'll drive by that store every day around that time, why not send me an ecoupon every morning at 7:15 AM? One that expires at 8:00 AM? One that guarantees that I'll have my coffee waiting for me if I accept the offer by 7:30 AM? All of these variations are readily achievable with some contextual data and some robust analysis of a few petabytes of data, daily.

Finally, Starbucks may go whole hog and shoot for Level 5 contextification, which is socialfied contextification. What the heck is this? This is where Starbucks monitors my social media presence and develops a deeper understanding of me . . . who I am, what I like and why, who my friends are and their likes and dislikes, and so on. Level 5 contextification implies a deep customer intimacy, one that is inherently intrusive and yet one that is so valuable to customers that they are willing to sacrifice some of their privacy to receive the benefits.

So in this example, Level 5 contextification would mean that Starbucks knows that four of my close friends also frequent that shop on Redlands Boulevard, one earlier in the morning, two later in the morning, and one at about the same time. Starbucks would know what each of us prefers to order off of its menu, as well as how we each customize our order (I like my bold venti blackeye to have room for milk, slightly cooler than normal, with one Equal, some vanilla, and some nutmeg). Most importantly, Starbucks would know how each of us *feels* about Starbucks, based upon our interaction with the brand at a deeper, more intimate level. Using all this knowledge, the Redlands Boulevard Starbucks could proactively set up a meeting for me and my friends, where we'd get a discount on exactly what we like to order and could meet one another in a social setting, all facilitated by Starbucks. Additionally, Starbucks could reward us if we gave them a high rating on Yelp, Facebook, or another social site, based upon the experience that Starbucks facilitated for us.

A further example of Level 5 contextification could be the roll out of "create-a-new-drink" contest at each Starbucks location. Each store would invite some of its most profitable and interactive customers to attend the contest, where they would each invent a new coffee drink. The winner would have his or her drink added to the store's menu and would receive some form of monetary award, as well as recognition for the contribution. This is deep customer engagement of the sort to which companies must aspire over the next decade.

These examples may seem far fetched, extravagant, or too sophisticated for other businesses, but this level of engagement, this level of contextification, is possible today. As such, your competitors are likely already here or well on their way toward reaching contextification Level 5. I challenge you to consider your business and your model consumer and try to identify how you might serve your customers differently if you implemented Level 5 contextification. Given that there are nearly a billion smartphones in the world today, I suggest that you move on these thoughts quickly, as the opportunity to innovate in this space is quickly passing.

The Contextification Imperative

Why bother with contextification? Is there really greater marketing power by buying into these trillions of markets of one? Will customers really tolerate the massive volume of marketing messages that will result from this transition? Time will tell, but all evidence currently suggests that the answers to these two questions are yes, and bloody-well yes! Look to the success of companies like Amazon, Target, and yes, Starbucks, as all of the proof you should need that contextification will be a game changer in business competition over the next 10 years, or so.

Perhaps you're thinking that you don't compete with Amazon. You don't sell books, you don't sell movies, and you don't sell ereaders, so you don't need to worry about how Amazon does things. This may all be true, but your customers are almost certainly shopping at Amazon or eBay or are users of Google or Yahoo. As such, the customer experience created by Amazon is the same experience that your customers expect of you, even if you don't directly compete with Amazon in the same product or service vertical.

It's critical to understand that innovators such as Amazon set the bar for ALL businesses. Even if you are in a business-to-business industry, not dealing directly with end consumers, you need to recognize this effect. While you may be selling your products or services to other companies, the people inside of those companies are themselves customers of companies like Amazon, and so they have the same expectations as your customer.

CHAPTER SUMMARY

1. Location-enabled smart phones are creating a market for context-based services. This market allows businesses to take advantage of thousands of daily context opportunities for the over six billion mobile customers in the world. Contextification will become the single biggest sales opportunity that companies will have access to in the coming decade.

2. Climbing the contextification maturity model leads to deeper customer understanding and, thus, greater customer engagement. This engagement means both more revenue opportunities per customer and the chance of greater profitability per completed transaction.

3. A significant challenge of contextification is to not overwhelm consumers with unwanted messaging. Companies that develop a deep understanding of their customers through data analytics will be better able to target their messages and offers to those context events where their customers are most likely to act.

4. To take advantage of contextification, businesses must prepare themselves to harvest, analyze, and act upon data at a scale that they have not previously engaged. This may include the daily processing of billions or trillions of records encompassing petabytes of data. IT infrastructures must be designed to cope with this dramatic increase in data volumes.

5. Contextification demands that businesses respond to changing customer needs on a second-by-second basis. In order to remain competitive, companies must reengineer their processes so that they can respond to these instant markets-of-one in an automated fashion. This means that customer-facing business processes must execute without human intervention.

6. Recognize that the effort to create your responses to customer contextification will likely require even more work, and generate more data, than the effort required to capture customer data. Your business processes must be reengineered to reflect this dramatically larger workload and the data that it will generate.

8

socialfication
the intimacy imperative

SINCE THE 1990s, companies have attempted to use technology to develop a deeper understanding of their customers. This led to a new class of software, known as Customer Relationship Management (CRM), that claimed to allow businesses to better understand their customers and further monetize their relationship with them. Twenty years later, nearly every company in the world has some flavor of CRM in place. These solutions range from simple contact databases to highly complex systems that track customer purchases, website visits, service desk calls, and other contacts. Regardless of their cost or complexity, CRM systems all have the same purpose: to improve a company's understanding of its customers and achieve a deeper level of engagement.

Interestingly, most companies have found that their CRM systems have dramatically underperformed when compared to the hype generated by their creators. While these systems may track a great deal of customer information, they are necessarily constrained by the types of customer information to which they have access. I can model a customer's purchases and try to use this data to better understand them, but can mere purchase history give me a deep understanding of an individual's wants, needs, and values? Can website click-through histories help me understand customers at an emotional level, or might there be a better way to engage with them?

By the 2010s, social media had evolved from being a mere technical innovation into a human behavior. It evolved from being a new means of communicating into a lifestyle. The scale and scope of changes to our society that are being driven by social media are still being defined, but there is little doubt that over time its impact may eclipse that of the Internet itself. Social media is affecting every aspect of our lives and the advancing application of social media into our lives, our Socialfication, will define the next few decades of our society's evolution.

Personalization, Participation, Engagement

Socialfication is all about the impact of our massive, real-time connectedness to the rest of the world. Social media sites, like Facebook and Twitter, are allowing all of us to form and participate in digital tribes; groups numbering from a few dozen to a few million people who share some sort of social interest with us and with whom we seek deeper engagement. Socialfication is fundamentally about the process of belonging to one or more of these tribes. Such belonging implies personalization because the tribe gets to know me, know my preferences, know my hopes and dreams, and anything else that I feel compelled to post to the group online.

Socialfication is also about participation, as social media is by its nature a two-way street. It facilitates, and tribes therefore expect, participation as part of an implied social contract. It's bad form to be part of a tribe and not contribute to it. Finally, these two trends of personalization and participation define the third characteristic of socialfication: engagement. By baring our souls to a given digital tribe and sharing our thoughts with this larger group, we develop a level of engagement with these people that helps us feel validated. The power of this validation should not be underestimated; it is perhaps the key differentiator between social media and other on-line behavior.

Socialfication and Business

If you doubt the power of this feeling of validation, you need only look at the popularity of social platforms in our global society. As stated, Facebook surpassed one billion users in 2012 and will certainly reach the two billion mark before long,[1] Facebook members have become hyperconnected, hyperresponsive and, as a result, hyperengaged. By hyperengaged, I mean that an individual with something to say can and will say it almost immediately, probably without thinking too much about it, and will say it in a way that can potentially reach millions of people instantly. Those people, in turn, are those with whom the individual has built a tribal relationship and, as such, has significant influence over.

Clearly, one cannot overstate the potential impact of such leverage. In our hyperconnected world, the unhappy customer will now "tweet" about a bad experience, potentially to millions of other people, and will do so the very instant that expectations are not met.

Once such a post is made, the customer likely receives dozens of responses from the tribe that either reinforce or counter the point, forming a dialog that may deeply impact that tribe's view of the business being discussed. As you've likely read in the popular press or on your own social media accounts, bad news travels very fast and very far in a socially connected world.

This leaves companies with little retroactive recourse and potentially substantial damage to their reputation. In response, many companies are hiring professional "tweeters"—people whose sole job is to monitor sites such as Facebook and Twitter for negative comments and to then respond as quickly as possible to each customer's complaint. Naturally this requires that the company collect and make sense of the billions of messages being created on these sites. Meeting this need to monitor and respond may outstrip the capabilities of many companies. However, being able to do so will likely be a key measure of success or failure for businesses over the next decade.

Socialfication substantially changes the relationship between companies and their customers. Today, this relationship is largely vendor focused, in that the vendor's efforts are spent trying to sell its products or services to its customers. This is a "push" strategy, where the message is sent out to the entire population of existing or potential customers and the vendor hopes that some of this message sticks with some proportion of those who receive it.

Conversely, in a socialfied world, the customer becomes the focus in the vendor–customer relationship. Through socialfication, vendors work to develop a deeper understanding of their customers, and then target their marketing messages in such a way that their customers are motivated to want the vendor's products or services in a very personal way. This approach creates customer "pull," rather than vendor "push," and leads to a much more satisfying experience for the customer. Additionally, this approach leads to greater profitability to the vendor, as well as a stronger bond between both parties.

An example of the sort of deep relationship that will develop between companies and their customers exists with Subway sandwich shops and their paid spokesperson, Jared Fogle. Jared claims that he lost 200 pounds on a diet in which he mostly ate Subway sandwiches. Subway picked up on this story and began to leverage it as part of its healthy eating message to customers. While Jared has become a singular spokesperson for Subway, has developed a degree of celebrity because of it, and apparently has a net worth of over $15 million,[2] such sponsored relationships between a company and its customers will become commonplace due to socialfication.

In the near future, companies like Subway won't sponsor one Jared; they'll sponsor thousands of them. They will sign up large numbers of customers who are also looking to lose weight and will track their progress in online communities. As they reach certain milestones while dieting, this army of Jareds will receive a range of incentives from their corporate sponsor, from discounts on products and services to micropayments of money or points that can be used for purchases. None of these customers will make the millions of dollars that Jared has, but each may earn hundreds or thousands of dollars from their corporate sponsors in return for their active participation in a social community.

The return on investment to companies that follow this strategy will be tremendous. Again, rather than giving millions of dollars to a single Jared, companies will give much smaller amounts to thousands of Jareds. This community will create hundreds of success stories, rather than just one, and will motivate even larger numbers of other customers to follow suit. The total marketing dollars spent will likely be the same, but the impact of these dollars will be significantly magnified as they are spread over a vastly larger number of community participants.

It is important to note, however, that with thousands of Jareds in the world, there will be a growing impulse to abuse the system. If there are dollars to be made, people will find ways to defraud companies that engage in this manner. The potential harm of sponsoring someone who is unworthy, lying, or a criminal will be significant. As a result, companies must put a lot of effort into checking the backgrounds of those whom they sponsor. They must monitor communications in real time and pull support the moment someone makes a misstep online. This will be the price of creating deep engagement with a digital community, but the benefits will more than pay for the associated costs.

As this example implies, socialfication will necessarily mean that companies must manage vastly greater amounts of customer data. It won't be enough to email customers coupons on their birthdays. Rather, each customer must be monitored in real time, with the company looking for opportunities to engage each customer in an intimate way. In the Subway example, if a given community member posts on Facebook that he or she really wants a high-calorie treat, like a messy cheeseburger, Subway needs to see this post and respond immediately, potentially circumventing the customer's backslide by sending a half-off coupon for a low-calorie Subway sub.

This example implies that Subway has built a mechanism for monitoring the posts of potentially thousands or even tens of thousands of community members, in real time, and to identify opportunities for engagement, also in real time. The amount of data to be monitored is potentially enormous (keep in mind that Facebook generates over 600 terabytes of data every day), and the sort of ad-

vanced language recognition that must be applied to get useful results from these data streams have only recently evolved to the point
where they may be considered effective.

Wikipedia and the Socialfication of Work

Anyone questioning the extent to which people will contribute their
time, interest, and knowledge for free needs look no further than
Wikipedia. As of early 2013, Wikipedia held up-to-date content
on over four million topics,[3] all contributed voluntarily by millions
of authors. These contributors received no compensation for their
work; they did it for nonfinancial reasons perhaps known only to
them. Nonetheless, Wikipedia has captured over half a billion entries by these volunteers and stands as a supreme example of what
can be achieved by socially connecting large numbers of volunteer
workers.

This does not mean that companies should not compensate people
for microwork that they may perform. Rather, it demonstrates that
nonfinancial rewards can oftentimes be sufficient to obtain significant value from those audiences you attract. I'll address how companies can take advantage of this process in Chapter 18, where we
will discuss the concept of crowdsourcing.

Proximate Markets: Influence as Currency

In Chapter 7, we introduced the idea of micromarkets, created by
the introduction and growth of contextification. One variant of the
micromarkets that is rapidly evolving is what I'll call a proximate
market. In the legal world, events have two causes: actual and proximate. As its label suggests, an actual cause is that which actually
causes something to happen. If you're hit by a car, the actual cause
of your injury is the fact that you were hit by the car. In comparison,

a proximate cause is one that contributed to the actual cause. For example, your injury may have occurred because you were hit by a car, but a proximate cause of your injury is the fact that the driver of the car was texting while driving and wasn't paying attention to the road.

The driver's lack of attention wasn't the actual cause of your injury, but if the driver had been paying attention, the accident wouldn't have happened. In the law, this is often known as a "but for" cause, as in "but for" the driver's negligence in texting while driving, the accident wouldn't have happened. The texting was the proximate cause of your injuries; the car striking you was the actual cause.

All of this is relevant in micromarkets because proximate causes, or influences, will become a new economy by which businesses and customers interact. If, by some measurable means, one customer, partner, or other party induces another customer to buy a product or service, the influencer of the transaction will expect and in the future will receive some sort of compensation. While a person who writes a glowing review of a product on a Facebook page may have done so simply because of a good experience with the product, increasingly that person will expect, and will receive, some sort of compensation for the positive review.

There is a wide range of examples of these proximate markets already operating today, but, in the future they will be rampant and will touch nearly every corner of the larger economy. As mentioned in the discussion of contextification, each event in which a customer uses some tribal and social influence to push the agenda of a company may lead to a micropayment in return. Companies that embrace this new method of advertising may find that the small payments made in return for positive spin in a digital tribe produce vastly greater results than those achieved through traditional, mass-market advertising. The mechanisms for taking advantage of proximate, influence marketing are already vast and are growing rapidly. Forward-thinking companies will embrace this model and will leap ahead of their competition, leveraging the addictive properties of social media and customers' deep need for a sense of belonging; even online.

Socialfication Maturity Model

As with the contextification model, the socialfication maturity model I am proposing runs on a scale from 0 to 5. Each level builds upon the previous one, and here the primary driver is the depth of social engagement achieved with each customer. At Level 0, there are anonymous transactions, where I receive no information regarding the customer's preferences or behaviors. As a result, there is no opportunity to engage with them. At Level 0, my customers and I pass like ships in the night. We've transacted business, but I haven't learned anything about them.

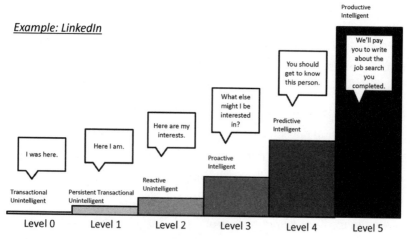

FIGURE 8.1. Socialfication Maturity Model

At Level 1, I am able to track individual customer behavior and preferences by his or her use of frequent buyer cards and credit cards or because the customer has "liked" or "friended" me on my social media site, occasionally posting these thoughts. Since I can attribute those interactions to a given customer, I can begin to model preferences and personalize my messaging. If you're company isn't at least at Level 1 socialfication by now, you're probably wondering what is this whole Facebook thing, anyway.

With Level 2 socialfication, I can start to react to customer needs. This implies that I'm monitoring my own site or that of others, as I look for comments regarding my company. So, perhaps your company's website invites customer interaction with online blogs or other social media postings. Alternatively, you may be accessing the message streams from Facebook or Twitter, looking for comments regarding your company, products, or services. When a comment refers to you, you receive some sort of notice and can then act on that message as you deem it appropriate. These comments may be good or bad, but either way you are reacting to them once they appear.

If your company isn't at least at Level 2 socialfication by now, you might be in deep trouble because it means that there are entire conversations going on among your customers of which you are completely unaware. Hundreds or thousands of people outside of your company are driving your brand perception without your guidance, and you are doing nothing to shape this message. Such commentary could be terribly damaging to your company's image or might be a source of great product innovation. Either way, if you are not plugged into these platforms you cannot respond to these customers nor participate in these discussions. By 2013, Level 2 socialfication effectively had become social media life support. Hopefully, you're at least at this level.

At Level 3 socialfication, companies begin to proactively engage their customers. By following customers' social media interactions, companies develop an understanding of their preferences and opinions and, as a result, can start to shape those opinions through targeted marketing messages. Proactive socialfication means that you are blending the social media data you obtain with your operational data and can start to engage customers as they begin each new experience with your company. If you're an airline with a customer who is particularly picky and also particularly verbose on social media, you can identify that person before his or her next trip and take steps to improve the customer experience before a negative post appears. Level 3 socialfication can be a powerful mechanism for managing your corporate image in the world.

At Level 4 socialfication, companies understand their customers well enough to start to be predictive about how they engage. For example, the airline might note that a customer told one of his or her relatives on Facebook about coming to visit. Based on that post, the airline might proactively send that customer a discounted fare offer, if the customer books the flight now. Here, the airline isn't just preventing a negative sentiment by a customer; rather, the airline is proactively creating a positive sentiment by predicting and meeting a future customer need. At Level 4, customer engagement starts to become customer intimacy that can generate significant brand loyalty and quantifiable improvements in profitability.

Finally, with Level 5 socialfication, the relationship between a company and its customers becomes productive. By this I mean that the company actually engages the customer in productive work, making the customer a virtual employee who is compensated by them for a work product. The airline mentioned above might actually pay a customer to write a travel log of the trip that was facilitated by the airline. With this level of engagement, the company has created a symbiotic relationship with its customer and begins to foster deep brand loyalty.

An additional example should reinforce this idea. Given its popularity, you're likely a member of the social media site LinkedIn. It is a business-oriented social media site where professionals can interact with one another based upon their experiences, interests, and business needs. It's a wildly successful site, and it is one that as of early 2013 had achieved at least socialfication Level 4. Let's look at how a user might interact with LinkedIn at each of the six levels of socialfication.

At Level 0, we might simply browse LinkedIn's site. We have not engaged with the site or any of its other users; we're there merely to perform some transaction. Perhaps we are looking for other people in our same home location with similar experience of whom we could ask some business question. LinkedIn allows this sort of anonymous transaction to occur, at least with those user profiles that are made public. So, if we ran such a search, we'd get at least some results, and our transaction would be completed.

At Level 1, we'd actually have an account on LinkedIn, but would not have provided any background information in our profile. By having an account, LinkedIn can track our activities on the site and start to learn a bit more about us. As I navigate through the site, perform searches, and use the other functions provided by LinkedIn, the site is able to learn what I am looking for and what I may be looking for. It can then push appropriate content to me, leading to a one-way communication path.

Move up to Level 2 engagement, and I have actually completed my profile. By analyzing my profile, LinkedIn knows where I worked, where I went to school, where I live, and so on; it would then use this knowledge to start to push content to me that I might find relevant. Users of LinkedIn will recognize this level of engagement, as LinkedIn starts to recommend other professionals with whom you might want to connect, based upon your profile.

At Level 3, LinkedIn starts to look for opportunities to proactively socialize with me. Based upon my profile and the connections that I have established, the site will start to recommend other people with whom I might connect (friends of friends, and so on), as well as other communities that I might be interested in joining, based upon my interests. This engagement increases the value that I derive from the site, as LinkedIn starts making connections for me that I might never have made on my own.

Level 4 socialfication has LinkedIn use its increasingly sophisticated model of me to recommend potential connections that are completely outside of my existing network of business associates. This profiling intelligence looks at my interests, sees those communities that I've engaged with, and may also tie into other data sources, such as what books I've bought on Amazon.com or what companies I've researched on Google. Aggregating all of this information allows LinkedIn to develop a much more sophisticated model of who I am, what I like, and what I might value, and seeks to drive this information to me in a predictive manner. As previously mentioned, some features of LinkedIn have approached this level of socialfication, and I predict that the site will more fully adopt this level as it works toward being a Level 5 site.

Another example of Level 4 socialfication would be how LinkedIn serves its other customers—retailers such as Amazon.com. I have noticed that LinkedIn frequently recommends books for me to read based upon my interests and those of my connections. If I go ahead and make a purchase from Amazon based upon a recommendation from LinkedIn, LinkedIn gets a referral payment. This would be an example of a predictive, or even a Level 5 productive, relationship created by LinkedIn for its users.

What might LinkedIn look like when it achieves Level 5 social-fication? Level 5 indicates a mutually beneficial, productive relationship between the site and the user. Since one of the productive outcomes for users of LinkedIn is making a job change, I foresee LinkedIn identifying people who have made career changes through their interaction with the site, and paying them to write up and publish their stories of how LinkedIn facilitated their changes. The user receives a payment for the story and LinkedIn receives kudos that it can share with the rest of its user community. There are certainly many more examples of how this model could be expanded, but this is the general idea of Level 5 socialfication.

Given that more than one in six humans now engages in social media, it is fair to say that this phenomenon has and will continue to impact every aspect of our society. Indeed, our socialfication maturity model shows that the impacts of social media are largely to be seen. Now that social media are a prominent feature in our social landscape, we will see them work their way into more and more of what each of us consumes every day. Companies that take appropriate steps to tap into our engagement with our digital tribes will extract greater value from each of us, and we will be happier for it. Companies that don't take advantage of socialfication will become more and more marginalized, as the loyalty that they command from customers will be eroded by a myriad of competitors that invest in the engagement imperative.

CHAPTER SUMMARY

1. By now, all of your customer-facing business processes should support at least Level 3 socialfication, if not Level 4. Likewise, all of your employee- and supplier-facing business processes should be at least at Level 2.

2. Recognize that socialfication demands the collection of, analysis of, and action upon gigantic amounts of data. This data must be used in as close to real time as possible, placing tremendous demands on both IT and your business processes. Further, all of this data must be stored and made readily accessible, due to the regulations and laws governing your particular business. Ensure that your business recognizes these challenges and has aligned its investment strategy accordingly.

3. By 2020, socialfication will be the chief determinant of customer loyalty, and hence, revenue generation and profitability.

9

quantafication
the building blocks of business

EARLY IN MY CAREER, my consulting focused primarily upon process reengineering. Through the 1990s, I assisted many companies by analyzing their business processes and looking for ways to improve their results. My recommendations to clients could include removing certain process steps, foregoing excessive or needless review or approval steps, streamlining the flow of work products, and eliminating late-stage quality reviews and rework. During that era, process reengineering was a hot topic in business, and I learned a great deal about how processes operate and how to make them better.

One of the key things I learned is that the vast majority of business processes include several steps that add little or no business value, tend to slow the process down, and do not add differentiation to the end results. Further, most processes can be broken down into a series of subprocesses, or substeps, each of which creates one or more outputs critical to the final outcome of the parent process. For example, if you were manufacturing a car, you would need four tires to complete your business outcome, the car. An entire set of business processes support the manufacturing of those tires, but you are really only interested in the outcome of those processes: the tires that you use as an input to your own business processes.

Continuing the analogy, it likely doesn't make a big difference to you what company makes those tires. Rather, you want to get tires that meet your specific needs at the lowest possible price. To achieve this, it is necessary to fully specify the parameters that these tires must meet, including their height, width, and tread pattern; in short, all of the parameters that would allow a tire manufacturer to produce what you need. I call this process of outcome specification quantafication, since you are defining the characteristics of a quanta of business value, or a process outcome.

In physics, a quanta is a package of energy with specific characteristics. A quanta of light is a single photon that has a specific amount of energy, a specific wavelength, a specific frequency, and so on. Each of these allows us to fully characterize that quanta of light, and thereby understand it. Physicists would point out that this definition doesn't take into account Heisenberg's uncertainty principle, which states that I cannot know all of a particle's characteristics and position at the same time without a degree of uncertainty. While this sort of uncertainty can and usually does also apply to business processes, it's a bit too deep to get into here. For our purposes, quantafication is the breaking up of your business processes into well-defined units of input or output that are readily interchangeable with other similar quanta.

Quantafication is then a necessary step toward effective process management. If you look at your processes as a series of related steps, each of which produces a given business quanta that contributes to the process's end goal, then the quantafication of all of these contributing business outcomes is necessary to make your business process predictable, measureable, and manageable. Interestingly, these are the very characteristics that determine whether a given business process or subprocess can be successfully outsourced, hence our interest in being successful at quantafication.

Outcome Packaging

Packaged outcomes are the result of quantafication. A packaged outcome is one in which all of the pertinent characteristics are well known and meet a predefined specification. If the outcome in question meets these specifications, then it should successfully contribute to the business process for which it was designed. Following the tire example, I once specified that I needed 17-inch tires with 215 millimeters of width and a winter tread pattern. I can find and successfully procure tires that meet this definition. Each of these tires is then a business quanta; an item with business value that meets a defined set of requirements and contributes to the creation of an item of greater business value (the car). Once an outcome is packaged, it is readily produced either by your own company or by any other company with the necessary skills and capacity. In fact, most, if not all, of the outcomes that your business process consumes may be more efficiently produced by another company whose focus is solely upon producing that outcome. This is the force that is underpinning the surge in outsourcing over the last decade.

Outcome Orchestration

Hopefully, by this point we have established the relentless growth in data that is occurring throughout business. Quantafication necessarily adds to this trend, as we must keep track of all of the data that is associated with each business quanta. This is even truer when quanta are outsourced to another party to fulfill, as we must be able to monitor the lifecycle of these items as they are delivered to our business and consumed in our processes. If there is a downside to outsourcing, it is this requirement for greater vigilance over those outcomes you are procuring from outside and the attendant data management requirements that come with this oversight. There is also the need to properly orchestrate the delivery of outsourced outcomes. You must ensure that you have a steady supply of the outputs required by your own processes without maintaining an excessive amount of stock, which would also be inefficient.

This balance may be difficult to maintain and is the science of logistics which has grown in importance over the last twenty years. As business processes accelerate, logistics will continue to grow in importance, as any error in managing a supply chain produces ever-increasing costs to the business. I refer to this management of logistics in a supply chain outcome as orchestration, as it can sometimes appear to be more of a performance art than a science. Companies that are particularly good at outcome orchestration can establish a substantial structural advantage over their competitors. Hence, it is worth expending significant time and energy toward this end, and it is the data that comes from quantafication that make this possible.

The New Work Paradigm: Workers as Process Stewards, Rather Than Participants

Another impact of the explosive growth in business data is that the speed, scale, and scope of today's business processes make process automation an absolute necessity. It was not that long ago that business processes were largely performed by people. Forms such as orders, invoices, and service requests were all filled out, reviewed and approved, processed, and filed by hand. People were intimately involved in every aspect of how a business process was performed and completed.

Through the 1990s and early 2000s, extensive deployment of business process automation software removed people from the daily grind of pushing paper. This software encoded the routing and rules of business processes into systems that could run automatically, taking in new business transactions and pushing them through the process toward completion. Such automation allowed for business processes to run much faster, more accurately, and more inexpensively; it was the fundamental benefit of the billions of dollars that companies invested in business process automation software since the late 1980s.

An example of these benefits may be seen in the growth of the New York Stock Exchange (NYSE) over this time frame. The NYSE has invested heavily in automated trading systems since the 1980s. These systems automated both the purchase and sale of stocks, as well as the reconciliation of these trades in the back-end systems of the trading companies. Prior to automation, such reconciliation could take several days, as people manually checked each and every trade for accuracy and consistency, and maintained a running total of the stock portfolio of each company. As a result of automation, the trade volume of the NYSE grew from 11.4 billion shares in 1980 to over 444 billion shares in 2010 (see Figure 9.1), which is an annual growth rate of almost 13 percent.[1]

Process Automation: Enabling Modern Business

Through process automation, the volume and velocity of nearly all businesses have grown dramatically over the last 20 years. Figure 9.2 shows the indexed productivity growth in the United States from

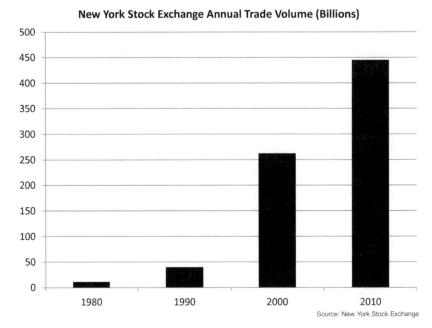

FIGURE 9.1. NYSE Annual Trade Volume

1959 to 2012. As this graph shows, the productivity, or economic output, of every employee in the United States has tripled since the 1960s.

In this, the information era, computers began to be integrated into our economy in ever-deeper, ever-more powerful ways. This arguably enabled this tripling of the output of the average American worker.

By the 2010s, this acceleration of business output has grown to the point that many business processes can no longer be performed effectively by people. People have become process stewards, who monitor the performance of automated processes rather than execute the processes themselves. People may still become involved if a given transaction proves to be an exception to the rules of the automated process as each exception must be properly managed. However, as the rules governing the resolution of each exception are defined, they can then be encoded in the automated process,

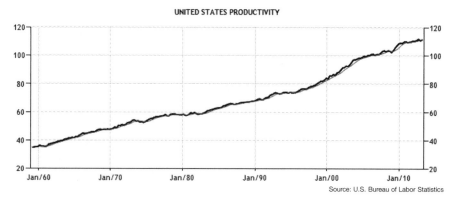

UNITED STATES PRODUCTIVITY

Source: U.S. Bureau of Labor Statistics

FIGURE 9.2. U.S. Productivity per Employee

ensuring that in the future they can be handled without human intervention.

This iterative definition of new business rules is critical to the ongoing optimization of automated business processes, as it ensures that these processes can accurately handle an ever-growing volume of transactions. Again, the role of people in these processes becomes one of process stewards, ensuring that the process is functioning properly and handling exceptions as they occur.

This trend explains the experience of contacting customer service for nearly any company in the world today. If you call the company's customer support services, you're almost certainly going to find yourself entering a maze of machine-generated questions that are used to characterize the nature of your query or question. The more information you enter into the system, the more likely it is that the system will be able to resolve your issue without human intervention. Solving your problem without such intervention is the measure of success for these automated systems, because it is several orders of magnitude less expensive than the participation of an actual person.

We've all experienced this infuriating process with phone-based customer support. The "press 1 for this sort of problem, or press 2 for that sort of problem" is all part of categorizing your issue in order to try to resolve it through process automation. Such resolution tends to be faster, more accurate, and much less expensive than getting a person on the line, and these benefits are why Interactive Voice Response (IVR) systems have become so prevalent since the early 1990s.

Recently, there has been an interesting reversal in this trend. Some companies have actually put people back in the loop of customer service, and they present this service as a quality differentiator. It will be interesting to see if this trend continues or if our continuing experience with automated self-service will change our expectations of what constitutes "good" customer service. When they are well-designed, automated services can be faster, more accurate, and more satisfying than those provided by people. Time will tell if direct interaction with customer service representatives (i.e., people) leads to a sufficient improvement in perceived service to warrant the greater costs involved.

Quantafication Maturity Model

Quantafication maturity is a discussion of how well-structured and understood your business's processes are, and thus how outsourceable they are. This is critical for determining which process outcomes are important to keep in-house because they are differentiating, and which outcomes can and should be outsourced because they are commoditized and provide no differentiation. Figure 9.3 presents the Quantafication Maturity Model.

As we have established, any outcome that does not differentiate your business can and should be delivered either by a commodity business that is completely focused on that outcome or by a marketplace where competition drives down outcome cost while also driving

Quantafication CMM

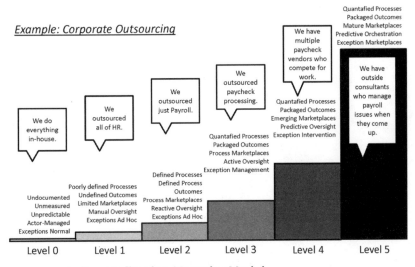

FIGURE 9.3. Quantafication Maturity Model

up outcome quality. I refer to this as the outsourcing imperative. Quantification is largely a discussion of process and outsourcing management. The degree of sophistication that is possible with outsourcing is directly related to how transparent a given process may be, which in turn is determined by information flow. Each level of quantification implies a significant increase in the creation, processing, and understanding of data. Let's review each of these levels in turn.

At Level 0 quantafication, we have business processes that are undocumented and are followed on an ad-hoc basis. Those who perform the process determine the correct way to accomplish it. Predictability and repeatability of the process depends entirely on the performance of these process participants. While these processes could be measured, they typically are not, which prevents their documentation, their characterization, and ultimately their outsource-ability. Finally, such processes are filled with process exceptions, since few people know what outcomes the process should produce. By 2013, relatively few businesses continued to operate in this manner holistically, since they would have been driven out of business by thirty years of process reengineering and automation undertaken by their competitors. Yet most businesses maintain internal processes that still operate at Level 0 quantafication. Classic examples of these "black arts" are marketing, product development, and perhaps, somewhat cynically, corporate strategy.

When we progress to Level 1, there is some process definition and some predictability for final outcomes. However, we do not have a good idea of what subprocess outcomes might be. Rather, the process is initiated and, at some point, the final outcome is generated. I've seen corporate hiring processes that worked this way. A hiring manager filled out a request that went to HR. Then, a seemingly random number of candidates went through a flurry of interviews at the end of which a position was filled. Such processes require a great deal of manual oversight, and there are frequent exceptions to these processes since their outcomes are fairly nebulous.

Further, such processes are served by limited marketplaces, because their operations have not been well defined and are not readily repeatable. If we go back to the recruiting example, companies frequently outsource executive recruiting to headhunter organizations. These organizations rely on their proprietary expertise, processes, and rolodexes (again, the "black arts") to find appropriate candidates and fill positions.

At Level 2 quantafication, a company has well-defined processes and reasonably well-defined process outcomes. Such processes are now outsourceable, and this is the present state of the art for much of the outsourcing industry. Many companies have entirely outsourced their payroll process, hiring process, IT helpdesk, and customer relationship management process. In these process marketplaces, entire business processes are outsourced, rather than subprocesses or individual business outcomes. The outsourcer pays for and receives a well-defined end result, but has little or no information about the interim steps that the outsourcee takes in generating that end result.

At Level 2, the outsourcer and the outsourcee review periodic reports of process performance, and the outsourcee is usually penalized if the contractual service levels aren't met. Such reactive oversight is common in these relationships. Also common here is ad-hoc exception management, in which the outsourcee independently charges for the management of exceptions as they occur. Again, this is fairly standard industry practice.

In Level 3, the processes are not only defined, but are themselves quantafied. Here, the steps of the process are well understood and create predictable results, or outcomes. In fact, many of these incremental outcomes may be "packaged" and are themselves outsourceable. An example is a company that is an outsourcee of IT help desk services. Such a company might have its call-answering process sufficiently packaged so it can route incoming calls to outside contractors rather to internal employees. Initially, such companies might follow this approach to flatten out variations in call volumes. However, over time, such outsourcing of packaged outcomes could take over all of the call volume, as this approach is cheaper and more efficient than handling the calls with internal staff. Some outsourcees are modifying their current business models in this way to improve their own profitability.

So, while Level 3 quantafication is showing some quantification of business outcomes, the benefits are largely gained by outsourcees rather than outsourcers. Farming out the work of packaged outcomes necessarily requires active oversight by the outsourcee, as it is still on the contractual hook for producing results at a certain level of service. Thus, at Level 3, we have active oversight rather than reactive oversight. Finally, the outsourcee should have achieved exception management, if only because exceptions must be identified before they are sent out as a work package to a further outsourcee. Such exceptions are invisible to the original outsourcer; they are entirely managed by the first-level outsourcee.

At Level 4 quantafication, the original company, the outsourcer, has regained control over those processes which had previously been entirely outsourced. Now, because the company has packaged its own process outcomes, it can outsource these process fragments itself, thereby harvesting the efficiency gains that were previously earned by outsourcees in Level 3. This will be possible because at Level 4, emerging marketplaces have developed for business outcomes. Companies have marketplaces to which they can outsource small, discrete pieces of work to be completed by individuals and organizations who specialize in that one business outcome.

In 2013, many such organizations popped up every day. Examples are 1800accountant and legalzoom.com. As these examples suggest, many of these marketplaces provide services that were once performed by highly differentiated, white-collar experts on a pay-as-you-go basis. The process outsourcees that created these marketplaces for their own use will be disintermediated when their customers reach quantafication Level 4, leading to the rapid demise of outsourcees whose business models were successful during earlier times.

Another characteristic of Level 4 is that oversight of processes will begin to become predictive . Companies that use outcome marketplaces will have sufficient control over their own processes and so much data to analyze that they will be able to predict their own demand for future services. They will use this foresight to obtain better prices in the marketplaces that serve them, further driving process efficiency and effectiveness.

Level 4 companies will begin to intervene in their own processes when exceptions arise. In the future, exceptions will be identified immediately and the rules for managing each exception will be determined and immediately enacted, so that each exception can be processed normally. Level 4 quantafication is largely a thing of the near future. We're not there yet, but we are heading there pretty quickly, and we should see the growth of outcome marketplaces accelerate and come to dominate many economic sectors in the 2020s.

Quantafication and, hence, outsourcing, is rapidly heading toward Level 5. At Level 5, outcome marketplaces will have matured to the point where they are highly developed and there are lots of players competing for your business. We will have moved from predictive oversight to predictive orchestration, in which the elemental outcomes of each process are farmed out to workers at maximum efficiency. As a result, each transaction is completed as quickly, inexpensively, and accurately as possible. The selection of each winning outsourcee will be determined by multiple factors, which will vary dynamically from transaction to transaction. This orchestration will become so important to overall business efficiency that it will become a key competitive differentiator. Companies that were successful outsourcees at Levels 2 through 4 might re-create themselves as developers of optimal orchestration tools, assuming that they survive the transition to Level 5 quantafication.

Finally, with Level 5 we will see the development of marketplaces that focus on the management of those process exceptions that remain. This will be new territory for highly skilled, highly educated, and highly experienced professionals who will be in great demand because of these skills. This will be the new frontier for professionals like lawyers, accountants, and engineers, people who can handle strange or difficult situations that resilient and flexible automated processes cannot address. Such exceptions will always come up and, as process automation becomes more sophisticated through analytic learning, the exceptions will become trickier to manage.

Necessarily, quantafication of your business processes will drive significant growth in the data that your business generates. Once you begin outsourcing your quantafied work, you will be integrating your business processes with dozens, if not hundreds, of outcome markets, each with thousands, if not millions, of potential providers. The coordination of these activities will require a very large volume of information transfer between your organization and this network of providers, both to initiate business transactions and to coordinate them through delivery to your business.

Nevertheless, the relentless acceleration of business will continue to drive the outsourcing market, and quantafication is the necessary step of making a business successful at this strategy. Indeed, I suspect that only those companies that invest appropriate time and energy into truly understanding how their processes operate and establish the necessary metrics for measuring their successful operation are likely to effectively use outsourcing to achieve strategic advantage.

CHAPTER SUMMARY

1. Look at your company's recent history as it relates to process reengineering. If a significant proportion of your business processes have not undergone a major reassessment and redesign in the last five years, doing so should be a business priority. Your goal is to achieve breakout performance improvements, rather than incremental gains.

2. By 2013, your customer-facing or logistics-related business processes should be operating at least at quantafication Level 3. If they are not, begin a plan on getting to, and through, Level 3 as quickly as possible. Supporting business processes, such as HR and finances should be no more than six months behind this migration timeline.

3. Where you have outsourced an entire business process, look to see if marketplaces are developing that will support delivery of the pieces of the processes that your providers offer on your behalf. As these markets grow, you should plan on migrating part of your business quantas to these marketplaces, disintermediating your outsource provider.

10

appification
instant customer gratification

I HAVE WORKED in and around the field of enterprise software for over twenty years. I have seen a lot of trends come and go, a lot of technologies wax and wane, but I have seen nothing in the world of software that has caused such rapid and radical change as that of mobile applications, or apps. While some examples of apps existed prior to the launch of Apple's App Store in 2008, it was Apple's introduction of an open software platform on its new mobile smartphone that launched us all into a new, appified existence. Of course, Apple wasn't the first company to introduce this model, but it was arguably the largest purveyor of this business approach, particularly in the consumer space. The impact of apps has altered the course of technology consumption over the last few years and stands to completely change users' expectations of all future software. Indeed, the App Store might very well go down in history as Steve Jobs' single greatest innovation.

One early side effect of apps and their place in mobile computing is a dramatic reduction in consumers' attention spans. The instant gratification provided by mobile connectivity, social media, and unlimited access to information resources has made our entire society extremely impatient. Indeed, we can think of this as the "appification" of society, where our every whim can be answered by the instant download of a $2 app. As this trend increases, only those companies able to respond will survive.

Thanks to this interest in instant gratification, consumers now expect a quick solution to every need. Many of these solutions can be very basic . . . which is fine, as long as they're quick and inexpensive enough to fulfill a short-term, immediate need. If so, they are likely to be successful. This, in fact, seems to be the present state-of-the-art in applications, as companies make their early forays into this new world of user-centric computing. It is not uncommon to see basic apps from literally thousands of companies, each of which provides some relevant information to users or potentially allows them to perform some basic business tasks. Updating your user account information or looking up a stock price are simple examples of this sort of functionality.

Alternatively, solutions that solve a range of compelling problems are likely to become woven into the daily lives of consumers and become a critical part of how they interact with the world. The uproar over Google Maps being dropped from the iPhone in 2012 was largely the result of the fact that here was a free "app" that became deeply ingrained in the lives of those who used it. The depth of this dependence was part of the rationale that Apple used to try to replace Google Maps; it is also precisely why there was such dramatic backlash over Apple's failure.

If you use a smartphone, you're likely familiar with this new paradigm. You've likely downloaded dozens of apps that were either free or cost only a few dollars. If you're like the majority of app users, perhaps 90 percent of the new apps you downloaded are going to have a dramatically short useful life. You may use them a few times when you first download them, and then stop using them entirely. They either served their purpose or failed to otherwise capture your attention. In either case, within a week of downloading an app, you're likely to never access it again. This is further evidence of the disposability of many solutions that customers will buy in the future.

If roughly 90 percent of the apps that you download aren't particularly useful to you, there is the remaining 10 percent that you find impossible to live without. You likely use these apps nearly every day (think Google Maps, USAToday, or Facebook) and depend on them for a wide range of daily activities. These apps rapidly capture the attention of users and deliver sufficient value to keep users coming back for more. These apps are particularly sticky and capture a commercially significant amount of customer eyeball time. The goal of any company must be to create apps that are part of this critical 10 percent rather than the commodity 90 percent.

The appification trend manifests itself in another interesting way: It creates a high tolerance for partial solutions and their ongoing evolution. Again, if you use apps on your smartphone you're pretty used to this. Nearly every day, one or more of your applications has an update for you to download. These may be to fix a functional bug that was found in the app, to enhance the performance of the app, or to add functionality. In any case, this constant trickle of updates and upgrades is a whole new way of doing business for software companies.

Historically, companies sought to solve a customer problem in a fairly complete manner with each new release of their products.

Users had very high expectations that the software they purchased was fully functional and bug free. Software developers spent thousands of hours testing and validating the applications that they only then released to the market.

This approach has rapidly become obsolete. Now, the trend is to quickly release a partial solution to a customer problem or demand and then to constantly refine the solution, particularly in response to real-time customer feedback. Consumers have readily embraced this new iterative operating model and have come to expect this process of constant, incremental, and most importantly, free upgrades. As a result, companies of all kinds must change their business model to suit this new expectation. Here then is another interesting effect of appification: users' tolerance of partial solutions. As long as my initial buy-in is cheap, and I know that there will be a steady stream of improvements coming in rapid order, I will tolerate an incomplete app. It's the new normal in software development.

A Software Development Revolution

The growing dominance of apps has led many users to rebel against big, integrated, complicated software applications that have dominated corporate computing since the 1960s. These enterprise-class applications, sometimes cynically referred to as crapplications, are difficult to use and inflexible. They typically work across multiple business processes and generate a wide range of business outcomes. They deliver the exact opposite of the experience created by apps, and more and more users will reject these large-scale systems because users have the daily experience of something substantially better.

Most of the companies that produce these large, integrated applications are responding by building apps of their own, if only to remain relevant to their customers. Many of these early forays into appification of enterprise software have not gone very smoothly. After all, these companies made their fortunes by creating large, complex, and necessarily expensive applications. The idea of creating small, simple, and inexpensive apps to achieve the same business goals runs completely counter to their entire business model.

However, apps are so compelling and are creating such customer pull that these companies are likely to make this transition simply in order to survive. Further, the breaking down of the functionality of large-scale enterprise software will parallel the quantafication of business processes that we discussed in Chapter 9, and the cloudification of business in general that we will discuss Chapter 11. As more and more of customers migrate to this way of doing business, the large-scale software vendors will have to follow.

The Next Application Wave: Concierge Apps

One of the enormous opportunities for business in the coming decade will be the creation of apps that manage other apps. Customers are already swamped with apps (nearly a million apps are available for either iPhones or Android phones, the two most popular platforms, and the Apple App Store passed 50 billion downloads in 2013) and many apps provide the same functionality, only targeted for individual companies or vendors. For example, I use two different customer loyalty apps for two local grocery store chains that I use. Functionally, these two apps are identical, as is the data that I provided to the apps so that they can keep track of me. The only differences between these apps is their branding and the deals that are provided by each of their sponsoring companies.

As users download and access more and more apps, it will grow increasingly difficult to keep all of those apps up to date with the users' latest information, preferences, and other data. This, then, leads to a growing need for app management. Users will come to expect their favorite apps to know them intimately, and to act accordingly. It will become increasingly important that these apps know when there are changes in a user's life—changes in their context, that is. This new family of apps will keep track of such changes and automatically update other apps for a fee to the app creator, of course.

As such, users will seek out tools that help them manage and rationalize the apps that they use most frequently, and apps that effectively provide this service will likely be able to charge a premium on both ends of the value chains that they facilitate. The market for such apps likely will appear rapidly, and early movers in this space will likely be the next "killer app" in the market.

I don't want to understate the extreme difficulty of this sort of context management. Anyone involved in integrating large-scale corporate IT systems like Enterprise Resource Planning (ERP) or Customer Relationship Management (CRM) should recognize the potential difficulties in integrating data models across dozens or hundreds of apps. Different apps will be built upon different data models, even using different labels for the same data fields such as address, UserID, or State.

However, the benefits that such integrative applications, perhaps called Concierge Apps, will be so great, and there will be so much pent up demand for this functionality, that their creation will be inevitable. These concierge apps will dramatically simplify users' experiences with their smart phones and will allow for significantly increased value to be derived from them.

Concierge apps will manage mundane life events, such as a change in address. They'll make such changes known to other apps so that they can remain relevant. Concierge apps will maintain our context in the world. The apps will also know that I'm about to go on vacation in Hawaii, and hence I'm open to being marketed to on deals in Hawaii, and so on. They'll know that I recently friended someone on Facebook whose birthday is next week and gently remind me that their favorite charity is accepting online microdonations in their name. Concierge apps will make navigating an appified world a little easier and will make managing our own context in the world more transparent.

Among the key goals of concierge apps will be to manage the flow of an ever-increasing flood of targeted marketing messages that all of us will endure in the near future. In 2013, I typically received about a dozen daily deals from Groupon, a similar number from Amazon.com, another 10 deal notices from eBay, and over sixty other deals from other sites. So, I get roughly one hundred offers every day from perhaps a dozen different websites. Few if any of these offers are contextified; they don't recognize where or when I am in the world. They merely make offers to me based upon my preferences or past behavior.

However, contextification is rapidly maturing, and most of us will be hit with contextified messaging over the next four to five years. When this occurs, the message traffic that each of us experiences will likely grow by two or three orders of magnitude. For example, if each minute of your day represents a contextified opportunity to sell to you, then there are almost fifteen hundred sales opportunities each day for each company. Hence, if you actively engage online with a dozen companies, you're potentially opening yourself up to many thousands of sales offers every day. If you think that you're buried alive by data today, "you ain't seen nothing yet!"

The impact of contextification is what will make concierge apps not just desirable, but imperative to your digital existence. Such an app will learn your preferences and interests and will route messages and deals to you that the app believes will be of interest. It will also learn what you aren't interested in (which may be more important than ever), and will politely decline these offers. Further, offers over-lap, the concierge app will start its own negotiation process on your behalf; pitting one local coffee shop against another in order to se-cure for you the best possible deal on your next latte.

Appification Maturity Model

The appification maturity model is shown in Figure 10.1. It begins naturally enough with Level 0. Here, your company has no app presence. As a result, you are invisible to the roughly two billion smartphone users in the world in 2013.[1] Given the forecasts for the growth of mobile commerce over the next four years, this is not a happy place to be. So, let's move up to Level 1 and start interacting with your customers.

At Level 1, we're able to push information to our customers via an app on their smartphones. This is identical to what customers

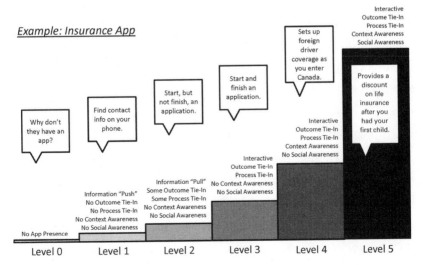

FIGURE 10.1. Appification Maturity Model

experienced with the first generation of the Internet; I can access static data, like news articles on the app from *USAToday*. These apps are simple portals into information selected and posted by the app owner. Such an app is relatively "dumb" and is reminiscent of the very earliest years of the Internet. Its delivery of push content is its entire purpose. It does not participate in any sort of business process and does not produce business outcomes. Naturally, such an app is neither contextually nor socially aware; it merely provides information.

At Level 2, we achieve a level of content targeting, in that users get to select which content they receive. This is content "pull" and is a fundamental characteristic of this level of app. An example here might be weather.com, where I can get the weather for a specific location by entering it into the app. More advanced Level 2 apps might also allow the user to kick off a business process, or create a business outcome, such as updating contact information or placing an order that would subsequently be processed off line (like many apps created by financial services firms). What a Level 2 app cannot do is drive a business process or outcome to completion on its own. It requires some degree of outside assistance to complete its work. As with Level 1, Level 2 does not leverage context or social information.

A Level 3 app is more fully interactive than Level 2. Here, we can not only start business processes, we can see them through to completion, hopefully in mere seconds. Many business-to-consumer companies have apps in this category. Such apps allow you to make purchases, pay bills, track a shipment, and so on. Level 3 appification is transaction oriented and allows you to perform a range of basic business tasks. Yet, again, these apps are not context sensitive, and they are not socially aware. They perform business tasks, but they do not apply any intelligence or analysis in the course of their performance.

Advancing to Level 4, we begin to have apps that are getting smart. Such apps are context aware. They recognize when and where we are and use this data to customize the user's experience. The simplest example of such an app is Apple's or Google's map app. If you perform a search on either mapping app and don't specify your desired location, the app assumes that you're looking in your immediate vicinity, your immediate context, and provides results that match that context. So, if you simply search for "gas" on a mapping app, it will show you gas stations that are near your present location. Similarly, some airline apps know at what time you logged into them and will present to you with whichever reservation you have closest to that time. Level 4 apps are convenient and intelligent; they begin to take advantage of the strengths of the mobile computing platform. By their nature, Level 4 apps are context aware. Yet, they are still not leveraging social data to customize according to our preferences.

This then introduces the key advance of Level 5 apps; they are socially aware and operate according to our preferences, relationships, and other social criteria. Such apps know that we prefer Indian food, that we have a frequent buyer card at ExxonMobile gas stations, or that we are fans of this or that sports team. These apps leverage the information available from our social interactions on Facebook, Twitter, and other social platforms, combine this information with our current context, and provide us with customized options from which we can choose. Level 5 apps are presently the best that we can deliver, although there is a wide range of potential capabilities within this level, depending on the degree to which they leverage contextification and socialfication.

Let's quickly look at an example of an app as it grows through the maturity model. Let's assume that an insurance company is looking to deploy a new application for its mobile customers. At Level 1, the company merely looks to push data to customers, so its initial functionality might list details about our company's insurance products and services. It might also provide some useful contact information, such as customer service phone numbers and email addresses, and potentially the location and contact information for the nearest agent or office location.

As this app advances to Level 2, it begins to allow the customer to interact with other corporate systems. Thus, it might let me update my account information, request a quote for new or additional coverage, and compare prices with other insurance companies. The app might even allow me to start, but not complete, the processing of a claim covered by one of my policies. Such a Level 2 app provides a greater degree of customer interaction, including the launching of basic business processes, but it doesn't necessarily allow me to complete those processes with the app alone.

By Level 3 appification, our insurance app is getting smarter and more integrated with my organization's business processes. Here, the app can not only start a business process, but it actually allows me to complete that business process through the app alone. So, not only can I request a new insurance quote, I can actually create the new policy and begin coverage solely through the app. If I need to file a claim, not only can I initiate the claim, I can see it through to its completion. I can even receive payment from the company through an electronic transfer in the app. At Level 3, the app begins delivering real value to both the customer and the company, as it simplifies their interaction with each other.

A Level 4 insurance app becomes context aware and, for an insurance company app, it might start getting a little creepy. Many insurance companies give discounts on auto insurance to drivers who do not drive a great deal. So, perhaps our Level 4 app would communicate directly with our smart car. Thus, if my mileage for a given period falls under a certain threshold, I'd get a discount on my insurance premium. Conversely, my smart car might notify the app that I have a bit of a lead foot and drive over the speed limit on occasion. The app might then warn me that if I continue this behavior my insurance premiums might go up (this is not likely to be a very popular feature, by the way).

I use the preceding example because it brings up an important point with contextification. What might be compelling contextual functionality to the company might be very unpopular with end users. It will be important for companies to validate whether a new function will be embraced by customers before it is deployed, as once it is released in the app, if it is unpopular, the damage is already done.

Finally with a Level 5 insurance app, we have achieved social awareness of the customer. Thus, if customers announce on Facebook that they just had a new child, the app might remind them to increase their life insurance—and give them a discount if they do so. It would also remind them to add the new child as one of the benefactors on my existing policy, and so on. Alternatively, my insurance app might notice that I am shopping for a new car online. As I search, the app could keep a running tally of those cars I find interesting and let me know how such a purchase would affect my insurance premiums. Again, I would need to allow the app access to both my contextual and social data for it to interact with me in these ways, but that is largely what defines a Level 5 app; it is both contextually and socially aware.

The trend toward appification has hit the marketplace with lightning speed. The only thing more surprising than the speed with which apps have entered the market is the speed with which the market has adopted them in return. There is every indication that appification will continue to dominate the world of software development and, indeed, many traditional software companies are now trying to fit their large-scale, complex applications into this new consumption model. It is almost certain that the software giants will make the transition to appification, if only because this transition will determine their long-term success. As such, it is likely that more and more of our leisure and business activities will be performed through apps on our smartphones, deepening our dependence on these devices.

CHAPTER SUMMARY

1. Review your company's current application development processes. While the majority of IT departments are still using the traditional "waterfall" approach to application development, leading firms are rapidly adopting so-called "extreme coding" or "agile development" in order to be more responsive to customer demands. Appification will force organizations to dramatically speed up their software development cycles, so drive toward adoption of these newer techniques as soon as possible.

2. Ensure there is an open feedback mechanism between your software developers and your customers. Because of appification, customers will not be shy about what is both good and bad about your apps. To drive rapid cycles of innovation, your software development resources need to be closely coupled to your customers.

3. Apps should not focus merely on customer-facing activities. Rather, apps can, should, and will automate and simplify interactions equally between companies and their suppliers, partners and customers. Ensure that your business is seek-

ing to apply appification techniques to these other elements of your business ecosphere.

4. Apps have extremely short life spans. Expect to refresh apps on a monthly basis and to retire and replace them on an annual basis. If you aren't adapting your business at these rates, you're likely falling behind.

5. Concierge apps will be a step change in the app market and will be critical to the continuing growth of appification. Concierge apps haven't appeared yet, but they should arrive in the near future. Keep an eye out for these apps and, once they appear, become an early adopter of this technology. Once these apps start to mature, their rate of adoption by the consumer market will make Twitter's adoption rate appear glacially slow by comparison.

11

cloudification
everything as a service

CHAPTER 5 DISCUSSED the now-mainstream trend of cloud computing. Most companies have either jumped into the cloud for their IT infrastructure needs or are planning on rapidly doing so. This is because the cloud computing approach has many compelling benefits, including reduced capital and operating costs, faster responsiveness, and adaptability. Indeed, these benefits are often provided by commoditized services in general and, as a result, more and more organizations' infrastructures will be commoditized and outsourced.

The outsourcing of business infrastructure and processes necessarily means that these outsourced functions require additional oversight—oversight beyond the support that can be provided in-house. As such, companies can expect to see a significant increase in their generation of such oversight information as they adopt more and more cloud-based services. This will require the creation and proper management of operational data that will grow in ways similar to consumer data within corporations.

As companies generate more and more of this operational data, they will increase their ability to understand, and then commoditize, their business processes. As processes become more predictable and more standardized, an increasingly compelling argument arises for them to be outsourced to other organizations specializing in managing particular business functions. The business of outsourcing is already enormous and is expected to continue to experience double-digit growth through the 2010s. Outsourcing is growing so rapidly that analysts at Gartner group predict that the cloud computing market will exceed $1.1 trillion by 2015.[1]

As more and more business operations become standardized, the commoditization effect will move higher and higher up the organizational value chain. It is common today for companies to outsource business processes, such as recruiting, payroll, and accounts receivable. In the near future, they may add logistics, fulfillment, and customer service. Again, such outsourcing will require creating, analyzing, and responding to ever-larger quantities of business data. This will enable business processes to be more predictable and thereby be turned into utilities. This expanding migration of business outcomes (quantas from Chapter 9) to outsourced, cloud-like delivery models is cloudification. And, as more and more of an organization's business processes undergo quantafication, so more and more of their business quantas can be delivered through third-party cloud resources.

The Eroding Value Chain: Commoditization and the Growth of Outsourcing

As larger and larger pieces of companies' processes are quantafied, commoditized, and outsourced, we will see an increasing erosion of their value chains. If a given outcome required by your processes can be produced more cheaply and easily by an outsourced provider, then competitive pressures will force you to embrace that approach. This piecemeal migration of work from internal to external production is "old school" with many lower value, nondifferentiation aspects of companies' businesses and will likely continue to migrate up their value chains over the coming years. This migration will be driven by both demand-side and supply-side forces, as companies look to offload more of processes and outsourcees seek to expand efficiencies of scale and scope. This migration process will advance relentlessly, and it is likely that many companies will retain only a small number of differentiating work processes in-house. Processes such as product development, marketing, and advertising, and, in some instances, manufacturing will be retained, with all other work being produced by outsourcees.

Middle-Class Mayhem: The Gutting of Services Industries

One side effect of the growth of cloudification is that an ever-growing population of middle management will be found to be redundant. Part of the efficiency created through outsourcing is the focusing and elimination of inefficient labor inputs, such as management oversight, reporting, or holding endless status or planning meetings. These tasks are largely the territory of middle management and have been the ground upon which millions of workers have made their careers over the last century. In today's accelerating, outsourced, data-intensive world, these roles are not only redundant, they are actually counterproductive. As a result, we will likely see a vast culling of middle-class, middle-management jobs through the 2010s, as companies struggle with increasing competition and dramatically increasing business velocity.

Many years ago, a good friend of mine was working on a consulting assignment with a major bank. He was developing software that would automate various internal processes, applying the banks business rules to the various transactions that occurred within its business. While my friend was working to automate these processes, he was struck by the fact that the bank insisted that many manual reviews be incorporated into these processes. He determined that the only real value of having these manual reviews was to ensure that managers of the bank still had a job to perform. He was pretty certain that if the software he was creating was properly designed, he could replace tens of thousands of the bank's employees with a few well-written if/then statements.

Flash forward to 2013, and this is precisely what has happened. In banking, as well as several other major industries, entire layers of middle-class, middle-management jobs have been cut, largely due to the process automation that has occurred over the last 25 years. For example, between 2011 and 2013 the following layoffs were announced in the financial services industry[2]:

- Barclays Bank: 2,000 to 3,500
- CitiGroup: 11,000
- Bank of America: 20,000
- Credit Suisse: 3,500
- Deutsche Bank: 1,900
- Goldman Sachs: 1,000
- HSBC: 29,300
- JP Morgan: 1,000
- Morgan Stanley: 1,600
- UBS: ~10,000

And so on. Naturally, these firms aren't saying that these layoffs are directly due to internal process automation. Rather, they typically say that these layoffs are the result of redundancies. Well, what makes a job redundant? One day your contributions were necessary and the next day they're not. Perhaps these companies are generating less business and therefore need fewer workers, but this is not borne out by their financial performance. In most cases, these firms are doing much better financially after these layoffs because they drive down operating costs.

Extensive process automation is a key driver in creating employee redundancies, particularly in process- and information-intensive industries such as banking. As more and more process automation has been implemented, fewer and fewer process participants are required, and headcount can be drastically reduced without impacting customer service. In some cases, customer service has actually improved through headcount reduction (back to the elimination of middle management). Productivity per remaining employee goes up and, assuming that those employees who are cut were the least effective in their roles, overall process quality also goes up.

This should be the case within business support activities, such as human resources, accounting, logistics, and customer support. Any business process that can be managed more inexpensively and effectively by an outsourcee will be outsourced. Competitive pressures will make this a business imperative. People who traditionally held these roles will find their positions rapidly disappearing and will be forced to take their still-valuable skills into the outcome marketplaces discussed in Chapter 9, which will emerge in the near future as the outsourcing industry continues to evolve.

Data-Driven Transformation: The Explosive Automation of Business

While many businesses have undergone significant business process automation since the 1990s, I believe that this trend has only started. Through the 2010s the trends discussed in Chapters 1 to 6 will lead to even greater automation, which will be driven by the need for greater efficiency and greater process speed.

If you have flown on American Airlines to Atlanta over the last few years, you may have noticed a Burger King restaurant in the terminal. This Burger King has something that I have seen in only a few other fast food restaurants: a self-serve ordering process (the adoption of self-service at fast food restaurants is accelerating). When you're ready to order, you step up to a computer terminal, click on what you want, customize your order if you like (maybe you want extra pickles), and then submit it. At this restaurant, a person still takes your payment, but I've seen other restaurants where you pay by yourself. In a couple of minutes, your order is delivered to you by whomever is completing the requests, as Burger King has not figured out how to automate the assembly of a hamburger.

Upon reflection, this process was very satisfying. I got exactly what I ordered, quickly, without errors and without having to help the clerk figure out my correct change. The fact that I became a process participant and replaced one worker by performing the job myself actually added to my customer experience rather than de-tracted from it. That the transaction was faster, allowed for custom-ization by the customer, collected more personalized information about the customer, and was cheaper to perform are just some of the benefits to Burger King. The only thing that surprises me is that Burger King hasn't implemented this process in more restaurants. The increasing minimum wage will accelerate the transition.

The market trends strongly indicate that we will see more and more self-service, as it becomes the new normal. In a 2012 study by Cisco, 61 percent of consumers surveyed stated that they prefer self-service checkout in their shopping experience. Clearly, businesses are responding to this preference. Thousands of Blockbuster movie stores have been replaced by RedBox DVD self-service kiosks now located in most major grocery stores in America. Those same groceries in America also now have self-service lines, as do retailers such as Walmart, Home Depot, and Lowes. More and more of our business transactions will occur with little or no human intervention. They will be self-serve, they will be automated, they will be fast, and they will be accurate. Additionally, more and more of these transactions will be initiated, managed, and completed by our smartphones and other personal service devices, potentially leading to the end of checkout lines. These benefits will come to be expected in all of our customer service experiences, which will accelerate this trend.

Cloudification: Outsourcing Everything, or EaaS (Everything as a Service)

As a growing proportion of a company's business processes are automated and quantafied, a greater proportion of them become outsourceable. That is, the process of automation creates a layer of abstraction, or a disconnect, between a request and its fulfillment. If fulfillment is automated and quantafied, anyone with the necessary automation can fulfill a request; it's simply a matter of proper data management during the handoff. This is why I'm writing about cloud computing in a book about data growth. Cloud computing is only possible because of the extensive automation of business processes since the 1990s, and using cloud computing necessarily means that your processes will generate more data—potentially a lot more data.

We've established that cloud computing introduces many advantages to businesses of every size. They include scalability, flexibility, speed, and resiliency. So why stop at computing? Why not apply the principles of cloud computing to all of your business processes? This is fundamentally what outsourcing is all about. The idea that once a business process is properly automated and properly abstracted, any portion of it may be outsourced for someone else to perform. Some business processes provide substantial differentiation to a company and should not be given to someone else to fulfill. However, these critical processes could still benefit from the automation and abstraction required for outsourcing, even if their fulfillment is maintained in-house.

Cloudification Maturity Model

The Cloudification maturity model shown in Figure 11.1 is closely aligned to the quantafication maturity model. Indeed, until a unit of business value is quantafied, it cannot be placed in a cloud solution. Quantafication is the process by which a business outcome is packaged so that it can be delivered by an outside resource. Cloudification is the process of actually delivering that outcome with prepackaged resources. With this relationship in mind, let's review the levels of cloudification maturity and see how these packaged resources may be organized.

At cloudification Level 0, we have delivery resources that are dedicated to a particular business outcome. These resources are assigned in such a way that they are only capable of delivering that one type of outcome, regardless of how much demand there is for the outcome. As a result, these resources may at times be underutilized or at other times may be insufficient to meet demand, depending on how much of the business outcome is required at any one time.

Cloudification CMM

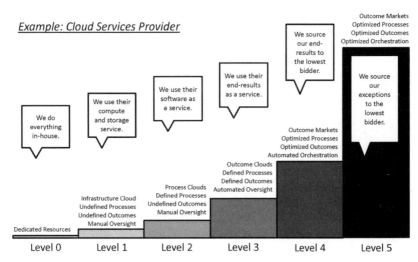

FIGURE 11.1. Cloudification Maturity Model

In the world of computing, this was the state of the industry around the turn of the century. At that time, a given computer program was typically supported by a dedicated set of servers, with a set capacity of computing power and information storage. On occasion, this capacity was more than what was needed, but the capacity was tied to this one business outcome. Thus, the excess capacity was wasted. At other times, the dedicated capacity might not be sufficient to keep up with demand for the outcome. In these instances, the business suffers as either some customers of the outcome are turned away or all customers must contend with poorer performance from the supporting system.

Today, when people talk of cloud services, they are typically talking about computing services: computing power and information storage. However, pretty much any resource that a business consumes can be delivered in a virtualized and abstracted manner, and thereby be cloudified. So, if we look at a business process such as payroll, Level 0 cloudification of payroll means that a company has resources within its HR department dedicated to the business process of payroll. These people and machines produce the single business outcome of payroll and cannot be used to produce other outcomes. By this definition, any business process or business outcome that your company generates with dedicated, internal resources is being delivered at Level 0 cloudification.

At Level 1 cloudification, the infrastructure that supports a business process has been virtualized and abstracted, which is to say that it can operate independently of a specific computer or set of computers. Because of this virtualization, the process can be moved to a cloud-based set of resources; indeed, anyone's resources can suffice. This is where much of the business world has been moving toward since the late 1990s. Companies are utilizing the computing capacity of third-party vendors to operate their business systems, but these companies are retaining control of the systems that have been moved to this outsourced infrastructure. This reveals two other aspects of Level 1 cloudification: first, that the processes operating in the cloud-based infrastructure are largely undefined and, second, that the business outcomes from those processes are also undefined from a cloud perspective. Additionally, the use of cloud-based infrastructure at Level 1 is managed manually. The determination of what to move to a cloud, how much capacity is required, or which cloud to use is largely made by humans in the loop rather than by an automated process. Again, Level 1 cloudification is where much of the cloud services industry has landed by the early 2010s.

When we reach Level 2 cloudification, we rise above the level of infrastructure and start to deliver business processes as a service. In industry vernacular, this is frequently called Software as a Service (SaaS) or Platform as a Service (PaaS). In either case, the systems involved support one or more business processes as a virtualized service, abstracted from the infrastructure or software that provides the service. The processes that are provided are well defined and standardized, although most providers allow for a degree of configuration or customization. These solutions do not support incremental outcomes, as described in Chapter 9 on quantafication, as these providers support the processes in their entirety, and do not allow subprocesses to be farmed out to third parties. Finally, Level 2 solutions require manual oversight, where one or more administrators must manage the ongoing operations of the outsourced processes.

There are many examples of level two cloudification in the market today. Perhaps the best known are Salesforce.com and Work Day, the former is a customer relationship management (CRM) PaaS and the latter an HR PaaS platform. Within these cloud services, customers may source and have the bulk of their business process needs fulfilled at reduced costs with greater efficiency. If there is a shortcoming to these offerings (and there are not many), it is that they allow for relatively little customization of these business processes, and they do not readily allow for outcome cloudification that is characteristic of Level 3 cloudification. Despite these limitations, Level 2 cloud providers have proven to be extremely popular, with the largest providers being able to claim many thousands of companies among their customers. A leader in this space, Salesforce.com, has enjoyed steady revenue growth since the middle of the 2000s, (see Figure 11.2), and there is every indication that this will continue until the mid-2010s, when the company may experience both market saturation and disintermediation, which comes with more mature levels of cloudification.

As mentioned, the primary difference between Level 2 cloudification and Level 3 is that at Level 3, incremental outcomes of each process may be virtualized and thereby passed on to yet another cloud solution that focuses strictly upon that one outcome. For instance, Salesforce.com provides functionality where its customers can cre-

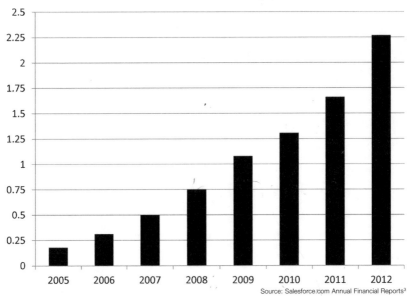

Source: Salesforce.com Annual Financial Reports[3]

FIGURE 11.2. Revenue Growth for Salesforce.com, 2005 to 2012

ate mailing lists. These lists may be exported to a program like Microsoft Word, where the list can be used to create mass mailings. Arguably, there is an opportunity for a Level 3 cloud provider to create a service that would take these file exports and perform the mass mailing for the customer. Indeed there are such companies out there, like Vistaprint, that provide a variant of this service. However, Vistaprint falls a bit short of a Level 3 solution, since the oversight of the process is not automated. That is, Vistaprint's mailing service is not seamlessly integrated into Salesforce.com's processes, and hence is not a true Level 3 cloudified service.

Companies like Vistaprint will close this gap very quickly, as such integration makes sense for all parties involved. Salesforce benefits by advancing its capabilities from Level 2 to Level 3 cloudification, their customers benefit by having more options for having business outcomes delivered by competitive third parties, and those third parties benefit by opening up their services to a marketplace that drives business to them. The value proposition is so sufficiently high that I would not be surprised if these sorts of services were established by Salesforce and other PaaS providers by the end of 2013. Hence, a key growth strategy for these PaaS providers is to create and support these outcome marketplaces themselves before their customers do it for them.

Outcome marketplaces then become a key differentiator between Level 3 and Level 4 cloudification. Following the previous example, Salesforce.com might create a marketplace for mailing list outsourcing where there are dozens of companies competing to deliver that outcome rather than just one. As Level 4 cloudification develops further, every business outcome that might come from the PaaS provider's platform may be supported by an independent marketplace, each populated by other companies competing for the end customers' business. At this stage, one of the primary value propositions of the platform owner is assisting customers in optimizing their business outcomes across these marketplaces. Indeed, orchestration of business outcomes across the platform's supported processes will be the true differentiator of the platform. Because of quantafication, outcome marketplaces will develop whether the PaaS providers support them or not. As such, it will be in the platform providers' best interest to foster the growth of these markets themselves, so that they can continue to control part of the process value chain.

Finally, PaaS providers will further advance their platforms to Level 5 cloudification, where the management of business outcomes across multiple outcome marketplaces will be optimized to the specific needs of each customer. At this point, PaaS providers will support fully customizeable, market-leveraged business processes that maximize the value delivered to end customers. As with quantafication Level 4, a Level 5 cloudified provider will also support competitive marketplaces for managing process and outcome exceptions. For example, if a company wanted to shop out the creation of a mass mailing and was concerned about the potential privacy concerns that might vary from state to state, it could find and engage an information privacy lawyer in a competitive marketplace for that exception.

The evolution of cloudification from Level 1 to Level 5 will take less than five years; such is the pace of business change in this day and age. This migration will occur both because of demand-side pressures from outsourcees, who are looking to improve their financial performance, and from supply-side pressures, as more and more middle-class workers are cut loose from their employers and begin looking elsewhere for gainful employment. Most of these people are likely to become freelance workers inside outcome marketplaces, performing their value-added work in small increments to whomever is the highest bidder on a given day. This change in career fortunes may be difficult for many, but then again they may find their independence to be more satisfying and their work to be more interesting. Time will tell if this prediction will come true, but we likely will see this migration occur prior to 2020.

CHAPTER SUMMARY

1. By the end of 2013, your business should be meeting at least half of its data processing and storage requirements through cloud-based services. Of this, at least half should be provided by outside, third-party providers. By 2015, these proportions should both grow to 75 percent or greater.

2. Beyond pushing infrastructure requirements into the cloud, your business should be identifying services and processes that can be pushed to cloud providers. Your use of business

outcomes as a service (OaaS) should be expanding as rapidly as your company can adopt these services, and by the mid-2010s roughly half of your business value chain should be delivered through such services.

3. Current providers of cloud services should seek first to migrate up their customers' value chain, while simultaneously looking to encourage markets that can provide the incremental outcomes that are part of the outsourcee's business. Over time, these marketplaces will likely grow to be the most valuable aspect of the outsourcee's business, so every effort should be made to foster their growth and adoption.

12

thingification
objects as participants

TODAY'S ORGANIZATIONS are under tremendous pressure to manage all of the information that is bombarding them. Our discussion thus far should make it clear that while the amount of data generated in our world up until this point has been enormous, we haven't seen anything yet. Indeed, if you apply a 50 percent year over year increase to the growth rate of data, in a decade you'd realize an almost 60-fold increase in annual data volume. The issue is, growth rates in the 2010s are estimated to be closer to 100 percent year over year, and accelerating.

Through contextification and socialfication, companies are going to have to manage the vastly larger amount of data created by the daily activities of their customers. While businesses are focusing a great deal of effort on understanding this customer-derived data, people as a source of data will quickly be eclipsed by a new source of data: things. More and more of the objects that we interact with every day are becoming "smart." Through the application of technology even simple objects can become aware of their context in the world, connected to the Internet, embedded with some degree of machine intelligence and thereby become participants in our global information network.

These things already include more expensive devices like cars, appliances, or homes. Things may also include much larger objects, such as power grids, highways, and air traffic control systems. Indeed, in this discussion of things, we must take a much larger view of what things are and what objects or systems in our lives may be made intelligent through the application of technology. As the cost of computing power continues to shrink, more and more objects will be connected to the Internet and become network participants. This process is already happening and will likely accelerate at a pace where objects that we would never think of as smart start to interact with us in new and surprising ways.

For example, some soda vending machines now monitor their own stock and will email their home office when they start to get low on cans of soda. Some cars on sale today can be started remotely by using an app on a smartphone. And, some airplanes actually fly themselves without any human intervention, including both takeoff and landing.

The computer industry is calling this process of making things intelligent "Thingification." As computing grows both much more powerful and much less expensive, our motivation to empower the objects in our lives through computing becomes more and more attractive. This process has deeply penetrated the manufacturing segment of most of the world's industries, where the vast majority of work that was previously performed by humans has been taken over by intelligent machines. This trend has begun to migrate into the world of services, where we stand to see yet another technology revolution that will put still more millions out of work—replaced by ever-smarter, ever-less expensive machines. Business tasks that used to require human intervention are now being performed by self-aware, intelligent systems.

This trend will affect consumers as well, where common objects in their lives, like appliances, homes, and cars will become intelligent and self-aware. In doing so, these objects will begin to monitor themselves and interact with us when they require our attention. In the near future, when you buy a new refrigerator, part of the installation process will include programming it with your likes and dislikes and then "friending" it on Facebook, so that it can send you a message when you're getting low on milk. Manufacturers have already introduced such smart refrigerators, and they can't produce them fast enough to keep up with the demand.

Thingification is driving the growth of a new Internet, an "Internet of Things," where automated devices are increasingly dominating the growth of data traffic on the Internet. This development is a boon to companies seeking increased efficiency and effectiveness throughout their operations. Obviously, a device that monitors itself and constantly reports on its own well-being will require less preventive maintenance, will cause less downtime, and thus will cost dramatically less to operate than a device that is not self-aware.

The huge volume of data created by all of these connected devices will dramatically increase the amount of data that companies can use in continually improving their products and services. The "Internet of Things" is already creating dramatic shifts in the economics and value proposition of a wide range of industries. Examples include smart meters in the utility industry, which constantly optimize how power is delivered to consumers, trains, cars, and planes that monitor their own health and "self-heal" until they are able to receive proper maintenance.

Smart devices are further feeding consumers' expectations of instant gratification and zero tolerance of defects or loss of service. This is certainly appropriate because such smart, connected devices do indeed create a new kind of intelligence, one that should prevent errors rather than just correct them. Companies that embrace this change and leverage the data at their disposal will become market leaders and will be able to charge a premium for the predictable, reliable results that their products and services generate. Companies that fail to make this change will be increasingly marginalized and will see their ability to meet customer expectations increasingly fall short—as will their financial results.

Thingification Maturity Model

The Thingification Maturity Model shown in Figure 12.1 will largely be driven by how quickly the functionality of RFID tags grows and how quickly their cost drops over the coming decade. Certainly the more expensive objects in our lives are going to grow smarter and more self-aware in the near future (like smart cars, smart appliances, and smart pets). However, we will experience a real revolution in thingification when RFID tags are sufficiently cheap and ubiquitous that the trivial things in our lives start to become networked. For example, when not only our refrigerator but all of the groceries inside it are tied into the network, we will see dramatic changes in our lives. We will also see the creation of a hurricane of data that can and will be collected and mined in order to improve our lives . . . and to sell to us far more effectively.

One could argue that Level 0 thingification would be where all of the objects in our lives are "dumb." But this definition is extremely

Thingification CMM

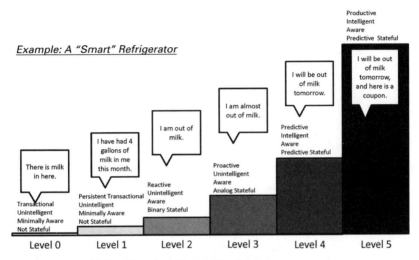

FIGURE 12.1. Thingification Maturity Model

outdated. We passed this level of thingification as soon as we began to put universal product codes (UPCs) on the things that we buy, allowing them to be monitored as they passed through their value chains. So, instead, I define Level 0 thingification as transactional thingification. By this I mean that an object can interact with its surroundings when it undergoes a transaction, or a change in state. So, when I swipe a box of crackers over the laser scanner at a grocery store, I can use that transaction to collect at least some rudimentary data: that is, the fact that someone just bought those crackers. The box of crackers is no smarter about itself than before the transaction, but the network has been notified that there is now something different about the crackers (i.e., they were just sold). As this example shows, our society is clearly already at this level of thingification, and so this will be our baseline.

If we were to look at an appliance that has Level 0 thingification capabilities, we might take a smart refrigerator, one fitted with a

UPC scanner so it can maintain a basic inventory of its contents by scanning every item placed inside it. This level of thingification is fairly dumb; it doesn't know how much of each item it contains or the state of each item (for example, has it expired yet?). This smart refrigerator has minimal awareness of its surroundings and contents. And yet, it does have greater awareness of itself than does a present-day refrigerator, and hence it is minimally thingified.

At Level 1 thingification, we get a bit smarter. Here our refrigerator can actually tell the difference between gallons of milk through some mechanism for making each gallon unique. Alternatively, this could be achieved by having a refrigerator that communicates with a smart recycling bin. When the milk container is removed from the refrigerator and ends up in the bin, the refrigerator "knows" that the next milk container that is placed inside of it is probably a new container.

Such a smart refrigerator has reached Level 1 because it has transaction persistence. That is, it can keep track of each transaction with which it participates. From this information, a smart refrigerator would know that you go through 4.2 gallons of milk per month, for instance. This information could be useful both to you and, naturally, to people who are interested in selling you milk. A Level 1 thing is still unintelligent; it does not keep track of object state (expired or not) and is minimally self-aware.

Moving up to Level 2 thingification, we start to achieve a level of awareness. Here, the smart refrigerator can determine that you have run out of milk. It is still unintelligent as it cannot "learn" from this information, but it at least begins to add value to you as the object's owner. Such a refrigerator is aware of the state of the objects it contains in a binary, yes-or-no fashion. By this I mean that the refrigerator would know whether or not your yogurt, your milk, or your hotdogs have expired. It would know if you were out of orange juice or out of carrots, and so on. In this manner the refrigerator is reactive; it can only respond to the yes-or-no state of an object. So, although the refrigerator is still unintelligent, its awareness of its surroundings adds to its value.

Moving up to Level 3 thingification, the refrigerator is now able to tell the state of other objects in an analog fashion. By this I mean that it can understand that your soda is half-full or that your cheese has five more days until it expires. The refrigerator can determine more than just the binary state (yes or no) of other objects; it can tell other objects' state on a sliding scale. This analog capability allows a Level 3 thing to be proactive. Your refrigerator can now tell that you're almost out of milk and should buy some more. It would know that the chicken that you bought three days ago is about to go bad, so you should use it today, and so on.

These determinations still do not require machine intelligence. Rather, they require a slightly more advanced level of real-time data collection. To determine if the milk container is almost empty, perhaps each shelf in the refrigerator has a weight scale that measures objects on the shelf before and after you remove something. Using this data and a knowledge of what you took out, the fridge can easily determine that you are about to run out of that item and send you a tweet to notify you of the impending shortage.

At Level 4 thingification, we have finally reached a level of machine intelligence. Such a refrigerator is capable of learning our habits; it then applies this knowledge to predict future events. Here, the fridge knows how much milk is left and, based on my previous rate of milk consumption, can determine how much longer it will be until I use up what is left. Level 4 uses machine intelligence and historical data to become predictive. This is a potential boon to users who don't have time to keep track of all of the items in their busy lives.

Finally, at Level 5 thingification, the things in our lives actually become productive for us. Continuing the refrigerator analogy, a Level 5 fridge would not only know that I'm about to run out of milk, it would also go online, search for the best deal on milk in my neighborhood, download an ecoupon for the milk, and then send the coupon to my smart phone in an appointment, telling me when and where to go to pick up the milk. Level 5 things start to act as their owner's agent—recognizing when they should take action and then doing so in an optimized fashion. My Level 5 smart car will know that I'm going to run out of gas on the trip that I am currently on and shops for the best deal on gas for me while I'm on the way to my destination. My smart toaster checks the humidity of the bread that I am toasting, recognizes that the bread is a couple of days from going stale, and proactively finds an ecoupon for bread on my be-half. Level 5 smart things will greatly simplify our lives, although with so much being predetermined before you go shopping, they may take a lot of the amusement out of going to the store.

Despite the "thing" in thingification, this process does not apply only to objects. Indeed, anything that creates a business outcome may be thingified; hence the potential crossover between thingification and quantafication. Examples of nonobjects being thingified include the deployment of smart meters in the utilities industry. Certainly, the meters are being made smarter; they're being thingified. But, as a result of their thingification, smart meters are thereby thingifying electricity, which is a service.

If business outcomes can be thingified, then there is no limit to the new markets that will be formed for products and services because of thingification. Hence, in the near future, we will likely be bombarded by new products and services that will make our lives dramatically more comfortable and enjoyable, all because of this trend.

While the thingification maturity model does not take into account socialfication, this does not mean that socialfication will not play into the thingification revolution. Rather, thingification can be combined with socialfication at each incremental level, creating even greater opportunities for machine or service intelligence. For example, let's say that we have a smart checking account, one that has undergone both thingification and socialfication. Through thingification the account is aware of the economy of me: my income flow and my spending habits. It would recognize both my fixed expenses (mortgage, car payment, electric bill, groceries, etc.) and the spending that's discretionary (dining out, going to the movies, etc.). As such, a really smart, Level 5 checking account could actually predict when I was about to spend too much money and could actually *prevent me from doing so.* So much for overdraft fees going to the bank!

Let's take this same smart checking account and now socialfy it. Let's allow the account to keep track of what I'm doing on the web. It would know what I am shopping for on Amazon or eBay or another merchant site and would also know whether the item that I'm looking at would fit within a budget that I preset in the account. If I'm browsing for tablet computers online and the cost of the tablet that I try to buy is beyond the limits that I set in my smart budget, the account would actually prevent me from making the purchase. At least, it would chastise me for buying it if I did. Further, if an item that I'm looking to buy is beyond my present budget constraints, a really smart checking account would launch a shopping agent online and start negotiating with online merchants in order to find me that item at a price that actually does fit within my budget. The agent would go through auctions, reverse-auctions, Groupons, and reverse-Groupons, ad nauseum until it either found a price that I could afford for the item or gave up trying. Either way, the intelligence built into the account would save me a world of time, effort, and focus with managing my personal finances.

Our refrigerator could also become socialfied, making it far more intelligent and far more useful to me. A Level 5 thingified and socialfied refrigerator could look at all of the items that it contains as ingredients. It could then surf the web for recipes that I could make with the ingredients at my disposal and look for those that match with my known food preferences. For example, maybe I like Chinese food and I have in my fridge all of the ingredients required to make kung pow chicken. The fridge would send me a note making that suggestion to me, which I could accept or reject based on my mood at that time. Giving intelligent, thingified objects access to our social preferences can lead to still richer functionality and greater customer satisfaction.

Unbeknownst to most customers, car manufactures have been thingifying their products for several years now. This thingification has gone beyond merely storing information in an onboard computer and downloading the data when you bring your car in for service. Recently, cars have become network connected through services like Onstar. These network services, collectively called telematics, allow car companies to collect data on your driving behavior in real time. Over the course of the past several years, these companies have collected petabytes of data on their customers' driving behavior: how fast you drive, how hard you corner, how hard you accelerate, and so on. They claim to use this information to design better and safer cars, and this may indeed be the case. But I have to believe that accident lawyers would simply LOVE to get their hands on some of this data when they have a client who has been in an accident.

Some companies have already used this drivers' data to improve cars already in service. For example, Ford has been collecting driver behavioral data for some time now, and it was particularly interested in collecting data from drivers of hybrid models. These hybrids use a combination of a gasoline engine and electric motors to improve the car's fuel efficiency. The way in which the car switches between gas and electric operation is managed by computers, and the logic in these computers can be changed by simply modifying the software in the computer. Ford originally programmed every hybrid car to operate in the same manner. Specifically, they were designed to make the hybrid operation as transparent as possible, so that the car mostly behaved like any other gasoline-powered car. This program arguably improved the cars' drivability, but did not maximize the fuel efficiency that was possible from the hybrid drivetrain.

Ford collected and analyzed the behavior of drivers of these hybrid cars and began to notice a trend; some customers were particularly interested in (some might say obsessed with) maximizing the fuel efficiency of their cars. Indeed, they appeared to be willing to sacrifice a degree of drivability from their hybrids in order to gain maximum efficiency. Using the data that they collected through telematics, Ford rewrote the software that governed the cars' operations and pushed this new program to those cars owned by customers who seemed to want maximum efficiency. This upload process occurred without any notification to the driver; it just happened (a great example of appification). From that point forward, those drivers who desired maximum efficiency were able to get it and most noticed a substantial improvement in the fuel economy of their cars. This then is another great example of Level 4 thingification, where the self-aware object learns its owner's preferences and responds to them dynamically.

An additional present-day example of a thingified device is an insulin pump. If you're not familiar with this device, it is a pump that diabetics use to dose themselves with insulin. Prior to these pumps, people with type I diabetes would have to check their blood sugar regularly and, when their sugar was high, using a hypodermic needle to inject themselves with an appropriate amount of insulin. With an insulin pump, the pump feeds a line into the user's bloodstream and users can give themselves a dose of insulin whenever they need it, without having to resort to an injection. The connection to the pump isn't permanent; the user needs to change the input site every week or so. But, the pump precludes users from having to carry a supply of hypodermics and frequently injecting themselves. The pump makes it far easier to administer insulin on an as-needed basis.

Recently these pumps have been getting smarter. Manufacturers have created electronic sensors that keep track of a patient's blood sugar in real-time. Rather than pricking their finger and drawing a blood sample every couple of hours each day, a person can insert a blood sugar sensor into their bloodstream that then constantly monitors the user's blood sugar. Naturally, the constant monitoring allows the sensor to become smart; it can look for trends in the person's blood sugar rather than just taking a measurement at a point in time. Such trends allow the sensor to predict highs or lows in the user's blood sugar and give the user an appropriate warning. Presently, these sensors do feed data to the pumps that users wear, but they do not yet directly control the pump. This is not a technical limitation; rather, right now, pump and sensor companies have not given the pump automated control of itself because of liability concerns. However, I suspect that with greater use of both pumps and sensors, regulators will become more comfortable with their capabilities. As such, it may not be long before the combination of smart blood sugar sensors and smart insulin pumps turn into a virtual pancreas—where a diabetic can live a life that is nearly as normal as that of a person with a healthy pancreas.

In all of these thingification examples, one thing should be clear: we are talking about the generation of simply enormous amounts of data. If your refrigerator is to keep track of everything inside of it every minute of every day and use this data to shop for you, that's a tremendous amount of previously untracked data being collected. Naturally, the company that sold you the fridge is going to want all of that data, so that it can resell it to the companies selling you food. So, General Electric, Whirlpool, and others will all need gigantic new data centers to manage all the new data that their smart products will be collecting. Further, the grocery stores that are vying for your dollars will also want access to your refrigerator's data so they can customize the best possible shopping deals for you and try to pull you into their store before someone else does. In effect, thingification is going to create entire new value chains across industries that were traditionally built on the sale of physical objects. As these objects become thingified, the data that they generate will likely become more valuable than the objects themselves. To survive and thrive in the near future, all companies involved in the sale of physical goods must prepare themselves for this torrent of incoming customer data, and realign their business models to maximize the value that they derive from this information.

CHAPTER SUMMARY

1. Regardless of your industry, you should expect that volume of data being generated through thingification will far outstrip that generated by your employees by the mid-2010s. Most of this data will be structured information, storable in databases, and will easily constitute petabytes of new data each year. Your ability to store, manage, and utilize this volume of data will determine your business' ability to drive innovation and efficiency going forward.

2. If you are a company that manufactures products, you should be defining ways in which your products may be thingified and determine ways in which to monetize the resulting data that your products generate. If you do this successfully, it is likely that this data can generate more profit for your business than the sale of the products themselves.

3. If your business is focused on services, look to ways in which making your services data-enabled, or smart, can add value to your customers. As with the checking account example, adding such intelligence to services greatly increases the value perceived by customers and can also reduce your business' operating costs.

part three

how successful businesses will respond

By this point you may be somewhat overwhelmed by the breadth and depth of change that this data tsunami is going to bring to your world. Fear not, because you can already take steps to not only survive this data crush, but to potentially thrive because of it. In this section, I present six recommendations for how to manage all of this information and how to put it to use in driving your business forward.

Finally, I close with a chapter dedicated to a preview of the future. Based upon the evolution of technology through the early-2010s and current trends, I try to forecast what the world might look like in 2020.

13

polarize
know thyself

IN THIS SECTION of Data Crush, I propose six steps that you can take to help your business not only survive the data hurricane that we all are experiencing, but to thrive under these new and challenging conditions. In each case, the goal is to either mitigate some of the pressure caused by data growth or to put that pressure to work for you in growing your business and remaining competitive. Each recommendation also sets some expectations as to what the new normal might look like in the near future.

Setting Business Strategy: Avoiding Strategic Dementia
The first recommendation is that you polarize your approach to business. This means that you must set your business strategy regarding how you deliver value to your customers, and you must be

true to that strategy. This choice is largely binary. Either you deliver value by being the lowest cost provider of a relative commodity or your business delivers high-value, customized solutions to fit your customers' needs. Choose one or the other and dedicate yourself to that strategy and you have taken a big first step toward success. If, however, you deviate from this strategy and try to play both sides of the business field, your business is likely to lose focus, lose employees, lose customers and, ultimately, lose the competitive race for business.

You might ask why I'm emphasizing business strategy in a book that focuses on data growth, as the relationship may not be obvious. But setting and following your core strategy may reduce the amount of data that you need to capture, manage, and learn from by half. In a world awash in brontobytes of data, cutting your data requirements in half can dramatically reduce the demands that data management is placing upon your business.

Albert Einstein famously stated, "Insanity is doing the same thing over and over again and expecting different results." Over the years, I have found myself working with or for a large number of companies that seemed to be suffering from insanity, according to Einstein. Typically, these companies had built their businesses on an efficiency-and-cost model. This means that they were providing largely undifferentiated commodity products or services and their focus was on internal operations: How could they become more efficient and drive out operational costs? If they were effective in meeting these goals, they could become more competitive and capture more market share, thereby driving up their revenues. Given that they were in a commodity business, percentage profits rarely went up by very much. However, total profits could go up with greater revenues.

This all sounds like good business strategy and, indeed, it was as long as these companies stayed true to their strategy. However, each of the companies that I have in mind longed for greater profitability, rather than just more profit. They wanted to somehow earn profits that were greater than would be normal for a commodity business, while maintaining a commodity strategy. In each case, these companies made some sort of move into value delivery, which is the strategic opposite of their primary commodity-delivery businesses.

These companies pursued their new strategy in a number of ways. Some purchased a smaller, value-delivery company and attempted to integrate it into their operations. Others tried to incubate new value-delivery businesses from within their existing operations and using their existing resources. Still others tried to create brand new business units from scratch, using all new resources and people. Through all of these efforts, these commodity businesses attempted to create value businesses using the same metrics, rewards, processes, and policies they had used to create their existing commodity businesses.

This resulted in what I call strategic dementia. If dementia is defined as a loss of cognitive ability, then strategic dementia is a loss of the ability to make rational business decisions because you are not sure of your strategy. So, try as they might, these companies could not help themselves from operating their new business units in the same way that they operated their existing businesses. They measured them in the same ways, they operated them the same, they staffed them the same, and they expected them to follow all of the same rules, processes, and procedures that had been established for their core, commodity business. Thus, they were doing the same things the same way, and yet they were expecting different results: the definition of strategic dementia.

I would argue that these companies were clinically insane, as they wanted to earn value-derived profits from their commodity-focused businesses without doing anything differently. Rather than polarizing, they followed a smear strategy by doing a little of this and a little of that, none of it particularly well. Needless to say their results were typically less than impressive. They all failed to see that the better they were at running their core commodity businesses, the necessarily worse they were at creating and growing a value-based business. Many of these companies would tweak a process here or add a sales bonus there in the hopes that these minimal changes would miraculously overcome the misalignment of every other operating method they had developed over years or even decades. However, to a person, the executives of these companies failed to realize that you can't transform from one strategy to the other merely by changing one or two policies or practices. And, you can't transform by simply acquiring another company that follows the different strategy.

Rather, you must realign every aspect of your business to successfully follow one strategy or the other. This is a necessarily difficult, painful, and expensive transformation to go through. If you do not make this fundamental shift from one strategy to the other, then you will necessarily create tremendous psychological friction within your organization. Your people will wonder which strategy is most important to the company? What behaviors are appropriate and which will be rewarded? Which business opportunities are worth chasing and, more importantly, which should be ignored? The more ambiguous you make your company's core strategy, the more time and effort your people will waste trying to second guess the questions posed above. I have seen this strategic misalignment cost companies vast amounts of money in inefficiency, waste, and eventually the loss of very talented people who chose to move to other organizations.

Not to overemphasize the misalignment of commodity players, note that I have also seen value players suffer from the same dementia. Here, I have found companies that provide high-value products or services start to deviate from their business core by trying to win commodity business from existing customers. The rationale apparently is that because the company has an existing relationship with the customer, they are able to expand their share of wallet with that customer, based upon that relationship. Because of their value-based alignment, the company cannot compete with pure commodity players on price. Yet these companies continued to pursue commodity business in the hope of increased revenues. The results of these efforts are predictable. Every time these companies tried to capture this commodity business, their pricing was substantially greater than that from commodity companies. So the value-based company lost the commodity opportunity nearly every time because of their misaligned price. Hence, strategic dementia doesn't discriminate, and every company has an equal chance of being misaligned with its core strategy.

Regardless of their core strategy, I found that these companies had absolutely no desire to actually change their business strategy; they just wanted different results. These commodity players wanted to earn the profits that are common to value players, but they wanted to stick to their commodity ways of operating. Conversely, the value players wanted to increase their revenues and somehow maintain their profitability by going after commodity business opportunities that simply would not support those profit levels. At these companies, I worked with many people who put tremendous effort into trying to meet these misaligned business goals; some were incrementally successful. However, these people quickly burned out by having to constantly swim against their company's main business current, and it was typical that the best people would only stay in these roles for only a couple of years before they became discouraged and moved on to greener pastures.

Strategic Alignment and Data: Efficiency Versus Flexibility

You may be asking, "What does this whole discussion have to do with data growth?" Your business strategy should drive what data you seek to obtain and analyze in order to grow your business. If you are a commodity business, your customer data should focus on predicting demand and on the logistics of supplying your products to your customers. If you are a value player, you should focus your data harvesting on actually creating demand. Let's briefly look at the difference between these two approaches and why it's critical to pick the right one for your business.

For commodity companies, the primary strategic differentiator in your business is price; you gain market share by being incrementally cheaper than your competition. Your data collection and analysis efforts should focus on finding ways to drive cost out of your business processes, thereby improving your competitiveness. It should also focus on making the delivery of your products to your customers more transparent and predictable, improving *their* competitiveness. Two forms of data will improve your cost structure: internal operational data and demand prediction data. The first is obvious. If you can reduce the cost of one or more steps of your business processes, then that savings contributes directly to your bottom line. The second category is less obvious. If you are able to better predict customer demand, then you can scale up or scale down the output of your business process in advance. This leads to better process efficiency and lower costs. In both categories, the goal of improving efficiency is the same, and both goals can readily be met through the proper collection and processing of business data.

For value companies, the focus of data collection and analysis efforts should be on demand generation. The company should understand its customers to such a degree that it can actually create demand for its products or services through advertising or other methods of outreach. Since no two customers are the same in the value-delivery space, creating customer demand requires that value-focused companies must be flexible in what they deliver to the market. Any action that contributes to operational flexibility will contribute to demand creation. Therefore, flexibility must be the focus of any value-based business.

An example of demand prediction in the context of a social media data feed might be to tap into the flood of data coming from Facebook to look for potential customers who are self-identifying by the posts that they provide. For example, let's say that you run a chain of pizza parlors. With some exceptions notwithstanding, pizza is largely a commodity. Each customer may have distinct preferences but the switching costs between one make of pizza and another are pretty low. If that restaurant chain wants to be better able to predict demand, it should identify from Facebook posts when a potential customer is contemplating a purchase.

How might you do this? Perhaps you could search for Facebook posts that specifically use the term "pizza." Further, you could look for posts between users who are asking each other if they'd like to get together for dinner. In those cases where you found such a post, you have likely identified a good target for a coupon or other deal. These Facebook users have identified themselves as potential customers who are about to make a purchase. If you act in a timely manner, you can intervene on their decision-making process and drive their demand toward your business.

Another good example of demand prediction is the subscription service provided by Amazon. With this service, Amazon allows customers to pick one or more items that they regularly use and arrange for those products to be shipped to the customer on a regular schedule. For example, if you use a gallon of laundry detergent every month, you can arrange for Amazon to send you a new gallon of detergent on a monthly schedule. Not only is this convenient for the customer, but Amazon offers a 15 percent discount for items that are on subscription, thereby further enhancing the value to the customer.

The benefit to Amazon is that it can predict customer purchasing behavior more accurately and consequently drive down the price that Amazon pays to its suppliers. Additionally, by setting up a subscription with a customer, Amazon effectively locks out other suppliers of the commodity items with which the customer has a subscription. Even if customers receive a coupon or other deal for an equivalent product from another source, they are less likely to switch suppliers because they already have a steady source for the commodity.

This is a brilliant example of using customer data to drive demand prediction. Here, demand becomes more predictable because you're actually capturing all of the customer's future demand for the commodity. Once Amazon has a customer buying one product on subscription, it is relatively easy to get that same customer to buy other commodity items in the same manner. Once I've established a predictive bridgehead with one commodity product, I can rapidly expand the number of items customers add to their subscriptions, thereby capturing an ever-expanding share of their wallets.

For value businesses, the goal is growing internal flexibility in order to be able to harvest the nearly infinite "markets of one" that we introduced in Chapter 7. Data relevant to flexibility comes from two sources. First, you need to collect data that specifies what each customer deems as valuable. This means the collection and analysis of vast quantities of contextification data discussed earlier. The combination of context and customer preference will reveal to your business exactly what your customers are potentially in the market for at any point in time. Second, you need data related to those business processes that you use to deliver differentiation and value for your products or services. Not all of your business processes will add differentiated value; thus, data from these processes are less important. Other business processes will be central to meeting each customers' specific demands, so keeping these processes flexible and ready to respond to just in time changes are critical to your business success.

A simple example here may be valuable. Consider the business of manufacturing cars. In a given production line, the vast majority of the manufacturing processes create cars that are identical. That is, 95 percent of one Ford Escort is the same as any other Ford Escort. However, that last five percent of differentiation may be critical to actually selling a car to a particular customer. If the customer has a strong preference for a red car, and all your cars are black, you're not likely to make the sale. The five percent of car manufacturing processes that make one car unique from another are critical to selling each car to each specific customer. Whether it is to add satellite radio, a sun roof, or high performance tires, these small custom touches are what make each car unique and of higher value to the customer. This is also why many of these custom touches are particularly expensive to add to a new car; this is where auto manufacturers make a significant proportion of their profits.

Commodity Obsolescence: The Efficiency Death Spiral

This chapter opened with a discussion of how commodity businesses seem to always chase after value-based profits, thereby leading to strategic dementia. I don't mean to put down the commodity business model followed by Costco and the like; it's a powerful model and adds greatly to the overall efficiency of our economy. Companies that follow a commodity and efficiency model can generate great business results, as long as they follow one simple rule: make sure that your commodity does not become obsolete. Costco, Walmart, or for that matter ExxonMobile, all are successful commodity businesses precisely because the commodities that they sell are necessities in the lives of their customers. Regardless of how technologies change, people will still need soap, hamburger, toilet paper, and gasoline, so demand for these commodities will likely continue to grow as long as our population and overall prosperity increases. If demand continues to rise, commodity players can earn greater revenue and somewhat greater profits by constantly improving their operational efficiency.

However, some commodity players are in markets where their products or services stand to be made obsolete by the innovation of others. Each new technology that we deploy in our society typically creates a wave of obsolescence that hits those companies that did not anticipate or prepare for the innovation. When the car came out, buggy whip manufacturers were in trouble. The arrival of cell phones started the rapid decline of pay phones across the world. Indeed, when was the last time you walked past a pay phone? Companies that used to produce TV tubes aren't doing too well in today's world of flat panel TVs, and so on. There are thousands of examples of commodity companies that, despite continuing efforts toward maximizing efficiency, found their customers disappear because of a demand discontinuity caused by technical innovation. This is a potential danger for commodity players; they may become so efficient that they drive the revenue right out of their business, or they may be so focused on process innovation that they miss out on creating the product innovation that leads to their product or service becoming obsolete.

A while back I worked for a company that was once a preeminent manufacturer of computer hardware, a darling of Wall Street, and the epitome of commodity-focused business strategy. When it came to producing hardware cheaply, efficiently, and effectively, no one came close to these guys. This strategy allowed them to sell on price and to open new markets that had otherwise been underserved by technology.

One side effect of their efficiency strategy was that its model focused on operational innovation rather than product innovation. All of its substantial intellectual capabilities were directed toward innovating how they operated in an effort to drive down production costs. This focus usually left them several steps behind competitors in terms of product innovation. However, this was not a significant weakness, as this company allowed its competitors to create markets for new products. Once these new market segments were defined, this company copied competitors' new products and captured market share by underpricing them. This strategy served the company well for the almost twenty years, during which the personal computing market grew up.

However, this same company is now in trouble. Its financial performance is down, the market for its core products is stagnant or shrinking, and there appears to be little that this company can do to stem the tide. How could the company experience such a rapid change in fortunes? It had focused so much of energy into driving process innovation that it almost totally ignored product innovation. As such, the owners not only drove the profits out of the business, they actually drove revenues out as well. They were so effective at producing the commodity that they made the product extremely inexpensive for customers to procure. This created a revenue death spiral, where there was less and less money to be made in the business, leaving less and less money to reinvest in innovation. Combining this death spiral with a step change in the market for the product caused by competitive product innovation left this company in dire straits. Owners found themselves selling an obsolete portfolio of products at deep discounts with little room for profit, which left little money to invest in trying to correct the problem.

The cautionary tale here is that if you are a commodity-focused business, process innovation is important, but remember to invest at least some effort in product innovation, lest you find yourself to be the most efficient producer of buggy whips in a market made suddenly obsolete by someone else's product innovation.

CHAPTER SUMMARY

1. Determine your core business strategy and resolve to remain true to it. If you are following a commodity strategy, focus your data efforts on demand prediction and customer logistics. If you are following a value delivery strategy, focus on demand generation using social media data in particular.

2. Identify metrics, measures, processes, procedures, and goals that create strategic dementia and drive them out of your business.

3. Where an interim outcome required by your business is misaligned with your business strategy, outsource that outcome to a provider with appropriate alignment. Build metrics and rewards around that outsourced outcome that ensures that the outsourcer is meeting the needs of your business.

14

accelerate
your only business imperative

AS WE ENTER the era of the data-driven, data-dominated business, one of the major issues companies will face is the speed with which things occur. Driven by hypercompetition, market transparency, and customer expectations, companies will need to learn how to act before their customers need them. They need to anticipate customer needs and proactively sell solutions in a just-in-time fashion. Data analytics allows such predictive action, but it won't come inexpensively or easily. A company will need the ability to capture and assess millions of pieces of data per second, most of it generated in real time. This data will need to be compared with huge volumes of existing data and with constantly updated models of customer behavior, also in real time. Once these analyses have uncovered a course of action, that action must take place immediately in order to capture the value of deeply understanding an instant in time for each given customer. And let's not forget that we must also analyze the results of the action, so that we can learn from it and continue to adapt our market responsiveness.

This whole business structure will further the trend of employees as process stewards discussed in Chapter 9. The volume and velocity of business will preclude real-time decision making by humans. We will no longer be in the loop, so to speak. Rather, we will be able to review the results of all of the automation that we've deployed and check on the health of automated systems and processes. Those astronomical transaction volumes experienced by Walmart in 2012, 200 million transactions per week,[1] will be commonplace for nearly all industries by 2020. It will be the new normal.

However, data analytics will enable this transformation by making our automation more and more accurate, timely, and proficient at correctly reading our customers. Simply put, the more data that you have and the more sophisticated your analytic capabilities, the better the outcomes that you can generate. This means that data-driven processes should become smarter and smarter over time, producing better and better business results. While many business executives may be uncomfortable with the degree to which they will need to give up control over their processes, the constant improvement in business results will make this transition inevitable.

Chapter 12 introduced the concept of "appification," in which consumers are increasingly expecting their wants and needs to be fulfilled in ways that are fast, inexpensive, and simple. As a result, companies are being forced to increase their responsiveness. Indeed, companies will find that their traditional focus on cost effectiveness and return on investment is outdated and that flexibility, adaptability, and speed are the new measures of business success. As with the other topics discussed, we will see how these new metrics will be enabled by and will feed an explosion of corporate data and what will be required to control all of it.

Given the short attention span and disposable mentality that is rapidly developing in our mobile, socially enabled world, a company's ability to analyze customer needs, convert those needs into a solution, and get that solution to market as quickly as possible will be the future measure of success. The sooner a company can get a solution, even an incomplete one, into an App and into customers' hands, the more likely it will be to capture market share for whatever product or service it is trying to sell. As a result, product cycles that used to be measured in months or years may quickly shrink to mere weeks or even days.

One need only look at software developer Rovio, the creator of the Angry Birds franchise, to see this new paradigm in effect. Rovio grew from a company of a dozen developers into a quarter-billion-dollar entertainment juggernaut over the course of three years.[2] It did so by first creating a compelling and differentiated product. Next, it constantly refreshed this product with small, incremental upgrades, improving the customer experience and leveraging the feedback that received from customers' use of earlier generations of the game. This approach enabled the company to not only bring new customers to its brand, but it ensured that the company continued to harvest additional revenues from existing customers. Existing customers enjoyed the frequent updates and refresh to the game, and Rovio maintained both its customer mindshare and its continued grip on its customers' attention and wallets.

In a time when software game sales had softened, Rovio's more than doubled in size each year, clearly showing the advantages enjoyed by those with speed and responsiveness. Rovio has become so successful, so quickly, that it even managed to ink a deal to build off of one of the greatest franchises in history: George Lucas's *Star Wars*.

This deal further fuels the virtuous circle that Rovio has created, where its incremental rollout of new game features and functions keeps its product fresh and entertaining, while building even more market buzz.

As more and more companies buy into appification as a business model and reduce their business process cycle times, they are feeding the expectations of the general consumer. We are all growing increasingly impatient in having our demands met and, with the wealth of choices at hand, most of us will immediately shift brands if we are made to wait for what we want or need. What was a competitive differentiator is now becoming a social force, and business survival will turn on whether or not your business can accelerate in response.

This drive toward acceleration in response to customer expectations will impact every segment of every industry. Examples already abound, and even the most common business processes are experiencing this acceleration. For instance, around 2010 the supermarket giant Kroger began an effort to improve customer perception by reducing wait time in checkout lines. Over the course of a few years Kroger reduced the average customer wait time from over 4 minutes to consistently under 26 seconds. This pretty dramatic reduction represents a substantial improvement in business performance. Looking at Kroger's financial results, it's clear that customers appreciate these improvements, as the company's financial earnings have been growing at nearly 10 percent per quarter in a highly competitive business.

Part Two reviewed six business responses to the societal drivers discussed in Part One. Of these six, four responses will drive the velocity with which all businesses must operate in the near future. The remaining two responses, cloudification and quantafication are actually enablers of the changes that businesses must undertake to operate faster. While each of the four is driving the need for greater speed in business operations, taken together they represent an absolute imperative that you accelerate your business. Let's look at these four forces in turn to see how they are driving the need for speed.

Contextification: From Demand Anticipation to Customer Prediction

Contextification, according to its maturity model, is going to accelerate business by forcing companies to at the very least actually anticipate the needs and wants of customers. Once companies can anticipate such demand and adequately respond to it, the next step is to actually predict customer needs and wants and to proactively engage customers at the instant they become aware of their needs. This ability is readily achievable with the proper deployment of technology. However, companies must recast their business processes to operate in this manner. Look at the processes you currently use to engage with your customers and ask if they are so sufficiently agile that they could become predictive. If you think that this is unlikely, then you really need to rethink and rebuild those processes to operate in this manner.

As you opt into the data feed of your customers' context, you should be able to see opportunities to meet their needs—perhaps even before they do. And, as I've pointed out repeatedly, if you can then you must. This predictive imperative is going to be the eventual result of joining massive quantities of contextual data with the advancing capabilities of Big Data analytics and machine learning.

Socialfication: From Hyperresponsive to Immediate Gratification

We already discussed how socialfication is enabling deep engagement with customers that will eventually lead to customer intimacy.

Part of what makes this relationship with your customers so powerful is that if socialfication is properly implemented, you should quickly move from being extremely responsive (i.e., we're so sorry that you had a bad customer experience with us) to being predictive. If you achieve this, you start to deliver immediate gratification to your customers. The moment they acknowledge that they have a need, you will be there to meet it. Once again, this level of customer intimacy implies that you have in place business processes that can support such business velocities. You may not yet, but it is highly likely one or more of your competitors are working on this problem right now.

Appification: From Business Value to Buzz Creation

By their nature, apps have relatively short life spans. For apps to be successful, they must provide immediate value to their intended audience, generate an initial buzz that drives their adoption, and deliver immediate value to the user. All of these factors require that you deploy apps quickly and update their form and functionality frequently, taking advantage of immediate customer feedback from their use. It's not enough to put an app out there; it is imperative that you constantly improve it to remain fresh and to keep customers' attention for which you compete against millions of other apps. To this end, your eventual goal for all of your apps must be to create and then maintain significant market buzz, so that you can continue to extract business value from them. This implies that those business processes that create apps, and those that are fed by the app, must accelerate dramatically.

Thingification: From Simplification to Result Production

Finally, thingification will also drive the relentless acceleration of contemporary business. At the rate of adoption seen through the

2010s, connected things will soon outnumber connected people, and each of these things will be constantly monitoring and acting upon their own status to the benefit of their owners. When conditions for these things require that they act, they will do so immediately, thereby creating an instantaneous business opportunity that will go to the lowest and most responsive bidder. These things won't make their decisions based upon brand loyalty; they won't be sentimental. Rather, they will respond to whatever deal best meets the needs of their owner that very second. Therefore, your ability to immediately identify new business opportunities and respond to those opportunities as rapidly as possible will determine your success in capturing these fleeting markets of one.

Here, we have four industry dynamics, all of which are demanding that you accelerate your business' response time. Multiply their effects against each other, and it should be fairly obvious that the processes that support your business today will be inadequate in the near future. What this means is that the old business norm of small, incremental process improvement has become a recipe for irrelevance. Improving your performance a few percentage points here and there simply won't work in a data-enabled market. Instead, you need to plan for and participate in productive destruction. You need to fundamentally rethink how your business operates, all of the time. Going forward, periodic process reengineering or even process evolution will be replaced with process extinction, in which old ways of doing things will be continually destroyed and then reborn based upon the application of real-time or predictive data.

Anyone doubting that speed rules business in this day and age need only look at the fortunes of Apple, Inc., over the last 15 years. Around 2000, Apple was in pretty dire straits. While it had a consistent three to four percent of the personal computer market, it couldn't seem to grow beyond this small core of dedicated followers. The products were okay, but they didn't show much innovation or the advanced design that we now take for granted from Apple. The company was even looking to be bought out by its arch nemesis, Microsoft, a thought that brought disciples of Apple practically to tears.

Fast forward to 2003 when Apple launched the iPod and iTunes. At the time, most people thought very little of this strategic move. After all, how was Apple going to grow into a tech powerhouse through digital music players? And yet, grow it did, setting the stage for Apple's next big move in 2008. That year will go down in history as the one in which Steve Jobs' genius was finally vindicated. Apple released the iPhone to a world market that was finally ready for a new experience in mobile computing.

The iPhone was a step change in technology. It used a touch screen rather than the miniature keyboard of the then-dominant Blackberry. It was sleek, modern looking, and, most of all, easy to use—a hallmark of Apple products. With the iPhone, Apple launched itself into a new age of growth that continued unabated for the next five years.

During those five years, Apple introduced the iPad, and the market sang its praises as consumers gobbled them up as fast as Apple could produce them. Apple brought out further generations of the iPhone, extending its lead in the race for smart phone domination. By 2012, Apple had become the most valuable company in history, topping $750 billion in market value.[3] Apple appeared to be unstoppable. But, like all mythical heroes, Apple may have had an Achilles heel in the form of its controversial CEO.

On October 5, 2011, Steve Jobs finally lost his ongoing battle with cancer. Throughout his struggle he kept a brave face, and clearly he was receiving the best care that money could buy, but pancreatic cancer is particularly aggressive and his fate was largely sealed. Since his death, Apple seems to have lost its way. The iPhone 5 was released in the fall of 2012 to a comparative yawn by the public; it has undersold expectations, and it has been reported that Apple has cut back on production capacity because of disappointing sales. In the meantime, Apple has lost its dominant position in the smart phone market to Google and its Android operating system, which is out-selling Apple phones by nearly two to one.

As a result of this rapid market shift, by early 2013 Apple had lost nearly a quarter of a trillion dollars in market value in just five months.[4] That's more than the total market value of Microsoft during the same time period. Talk about a rollercoaster ride! If you have owned stock in Apple for the last decade, you might be dizzy from all the ups and downs that you've endured. But, in today's world, such dramatic shifts in business fortunes are likely to become more common in the future, and they will impact an ever wider range of industries and companies.

Consumers have much better access to information than ever before, and they are also far more interconnected with each other. When a new product or service is particularly innovative, useful, or valuable to end users, it can go viral almost immediately. The buzz surrounding the product becomes self-reinforcing within the net-worked marketplace, until customers are practically lining up for the opportunity to spend their money.

An effect of cloudification is that nearly any startup company can immediately scale its business up as it builds demand. Hence, com-panies that are able to generate a strong buzz for their product or service can also immediately scale to meet the demand that results from that buzz. As such, traditional companies see their structural advantages of scale and scope continue to deteriorate. This will result in an ever-growing pressure to innovate in order to keep up with start-up companies that are no longer constrained by their relative lack of capital.

The increasing speed of business is nothing new. This has been a trend across all industries for the last several decades. However, I believe that we are about to enter an era where the acceleration of business will outstrip anything that we have seen in the past. This will make the need for business process evolution inadequate. Rather, it will demand business process revolution the likes of which we haven't yet experienced.

CHAPTER SUMMARY

1. Moving further into the 21st century, speed is life to an organization. For any business process that touches your customers, set the goal of cutting the cycle time of that process at least in half within the next 12 to 18 months.

2. To achieve this cycle-time reduction, analyze all of your business processes for points where your transactions slow down or stop. This will typically be caused by the need for someone's input, authorization, approval, and so on. Wherever possible, remove these input requirements from the process, either through automation or through reengineering these inputs out of the process.

3. Leverage social media, your customer call centers, and all other sources of feedback from customers to identify areas where your business needs to improve and use this feedback to define what those improvements need to be.

4. Look for and reward step changes in your processes, products, and services. When one is found, implement it as rapidly as possible, surrounding the implementation with metrics to determine the effectiveness of the change in generating positive customer response.

5. When a step change is made, work to create buzz for the change through social media and other digital channels. Making the change is not enough; making the world aware of and excited by the change is your real goal.

15

data enable

leveraging your most valuable asset

AS THE BASIC PREMISE of this book suggests, companies are finding that the data generated by their operations is growing exponentially. Unfortunately for the unprepared, this trend will almost certainly become more serious in the coming decade because of the cultural forces reviewed in Part One. The data created through business operations will represent a potential gold mine for companies that learn to properly manage and use it and will become a digital albatross for those who don't.

If the trends of the 2000s and early 2010s continue, companies will see an acceleration of the double digit year-over-year growth in data volumes. Indeed, today I work with some companies that are already seeing an annual doubling of their data volume. This ever-expanding volume will become increasingly difficult to manage, while at the same time representing an organization's most valuable asset.

Historically, most of this data growth has come from internal sources. These include both structured systems, such as Enterprise Resource Planning (ERP), Supply Chain Management (SCM), and Customer Relationship Management (CRM) systems, and more recently unstructured systems, such as Enterprise Content Management (ECM), Records Management (RM), and collaboration systems. By merging these systems, companies are able to develop a deeper understanding of their operations, their customers, and how their products and services are consumed. However, many companies have been challenged to merge the information stored in these structured and unstructured systems to create a cohesive picture of their internal operations.

The data generated by structured systems tends to grow linearly with the growth of the business. If a company's revenues are growing 10 percent per year, then its structured transactional data is likely growing at nearly the same rate. However, the growth of unstructured data in most companies is tracking closer to the rate of growth of social media platforms, such as Facebook; that is, they are growing at 50 percent or more year over year. This makes sense, because corporate collaboration platforms such as Microsoft SharePoint or Jive mimic the functionality of social media and bring it into the corporate context. As such, the more a given company begins to leverage collaboration platforms within its organization, the faster its resulting rate of data growth.

The issue of merging structured and unstructured data is one of the key challenges of implementing Big Data analytics, as discussed in Chapter 6. This is difficult because to extract new ideas and understanding from Big Data you need to combine hundreds of data streams from multiple sources into something comprehensible.

Companies and their managers are very comfortable in dealing with structured data coming from financial, logistics, or sales systems. However, most are far less comfortable dealing with unstructured data, such as that which comes from customer service systems, email, Facebook, or Twitter. Yet, it is the combination of these two types of data streams that leads to unique and valuable insights and represents both the challenge and the opportunity for companies able to combine these sources of information and use the results to transform how they do business.

It is in the vast and growing body of unstructured content that the greatest gains are waiting to be made. Given the richness of the information in these systems and their relentless growth, companies that set out to harvest the value from these data sets stand to gain a substantial competitive advantage. Further, sources of unstructured information are not limited to internal platforms; rather, some of the greatest value in Big Data analytics come from tapping into the data streams of public platforms, such as Facebook. In either case, companies that undergo this effort face a serious challenge in consuming and making sense of these data sets. Since most public social platforms are growing at between fifty and one hundred percent year over year, it stands to reason that social platforms maintained within companies should see similar growth. In fact, the Association of Information and Image Management (AIIM) estimates that in the 2010s, approximately ninety percent of the data generated within companies are unstructured data, in the form of emails, documents, blogs, and so on.[1] Further, they estimate that most companies are seeing growth rates of this unstructured data in the range of at least sixty to seventy percent, year over year.

All of this data growth means that a continuously growing proportion of a company's Information Technology (IT) budget will be dedicated to simply holding on to old information—a prospect that on the surface does not seem cost effective. Since legal and regulatory requirements force many companies to keep all of the data generated by their business, purging old data is not a viable option. Nor is it a wise option, since there is so much untapped knowledge hidden in this old, unmined data. As such, companies cannot and should not cull this data, instead they should put it to work. Those who succeed in doing so will begin to recognize that IT can be a strategic differentiator to the business, rather than just another cost center.

The Information Economy: The New Definition of Value

While most companies are coming to the conclusion that data can be the source of untold corporate riches in our present information economy, many of these very same companies have created systems that literally prevent their data from being used. In the 2010s, it's not unusual to find Fortune 1000 companies that are maintaining data environments with petabytes of information (one petabyte is a million gigabytes, or approximately what could be held by one thousand very large hard drives in 2013). Keeping this amount of information instantly available can be pretty expensive, particularly if this volume of data is growing at twenty percent or more annually. As a result, many companies place their older data into archives made up of thousands and thousands of tapes, as tape storage is significantly less expensive than online disk storage.

While this approach is certainly less costly from a capital expenditure perspective, placing data on tape takes it "off line." It is not readily accessible to analysts and therefore cannot contribute to a company's efforts to better understand its customers or its operations. Over the years, I have seen many archive locations used by large companies to save these offline data tapes. If you have seen the movie *Raiders of the Lost Ark,* perhaps you recall the very last scene in which the ark has been placed in a box and a worker is pushing that box into a warehouse with thousands and thousands of other boxes. I always think of that scene when I see the data archives of Fortune 1000 companies. In nearly every instance, the archive location is a gigantic warehouse filled with thousands and thousands of boxes, themselves filled with tens of thousands of magnetic tapes holding the company's old data. And just like in the scene from the movie, once a company's data has entered the warehouse, it is effectively lost forever; it is buried in a gigantic mountain of boxes.

Some would argue that much of this old data is not of any value, so there is no need to keep it online for analytic purposes. I have two responses to this. First, the analysis of structured corporate data in conjunction with unstructured data such as internal email and collaboration platforms or with external sources such as Twitter or Facebook is a relatively new phenomenon. As such, the likelihood that data more than two or three years old has been properly mixed with these new data sources and subsequently mined for new insights is extremely low. The fact that these data are maintained off line means that, by definition, it cannot contribute to the growing knowledge base of the company.

Second, the cost of storing data on either tapes or disks is constantly falling according to Moore's Law (which states that the cost of computing or storage capacity drops by half approximately every 18 months). At the same time, the volume of the old data remains the same, simply because it is old data and is not being added to without further processing or analysis. However, this old data can provide longer, deeper, and thus greater context to any analysis that might be performed by data scientists using company data, thereby making the results of such analyses more accurate and more relevant. Thus, here is an untapped resource that becomes less expensive to maintain every day and whose value as a basis of knowledge grows every day.

Data Efficiency: The New Watch Phrase for IT

The argument for placing old data on tape rather than disk is based on the fact that the disk is less expensive by perhaps a factor of three or four. However, this calculation completely discounts the potential value of the data if it were available for analysis. Given that data analysis is quickly becoming one of the key differentiators between successful and unsuccessful companies, I believe that the use of tape for the retention of data in offline archives is going to be recognized as financially unacceptable, if not irresponsible.

In addition, the majority of companies do not emphasize efficiency with the information storage systems that they build and manage. As is typical with the computer industry, there tends to be a great deal of focus on the performance of information storage resources, that is, how fast they move information in or out of storage so that it may be used. This focus typically overrides the concern over how efficiently the information is being stored when it is not in use, which is the vast majority of the time.

There are a range of tools and techniques available to improve data storage efficiency. Examples include:

- *Deduplication:* The automated removal of multiple copies of the same file.

- *Data compression:* The removal of redundant information within a file in order to reduce its size.

- *Thin provisioning of storage resources*: Allocating only those resources that are actually being used, rather than reserving more space than you need at that time.

I will forego a deep technical discussion of each of these tools, as they are well covered by other authors. But, given the rates of information growth that we are all certain to experience in the near future, it is absolutely imperative that companies use every tool at their disposal to reduce the volume of data that they are storing and to maximize the efficiency of data storage, rather than just the accessibility of data.

Quantification: Every Aspect of Business Data Enabled and Data Governed

What should be clear from this discussion about data availability is that it is imperative that companies capture and make available to the business all of the data that may help to characterize its performance. This requires two key steps. First, meaningful metrics for every business process in the company must be identified and captured. In particular, those business outcomes and processes that most closely align to your business strategy must be quantified through operational data, so that those outcomes can be monitored and optimized, as discussed in Chapter 13. Once you have ensured that these key business metrics are being captured, you must then guarantee that these data are readily available for analysis.

I use the term quantification to describe the trend toward data enablement of all aspects of a business's operations. Note that this is related to but different from the quantafication mentioned in Chapter 9. Quantification is the application of thingification, contextification, and Big Data analytics to deeply quantify the ins and outs of how a business process is functioning. The purpose of quantification is to use these new tools and processes to automate not only the operation of your business processes, but to also automate the ongoing evolution of those same processes.

Certainly, companies have been collecting data on their operations for several decades. However, the merging of transactional data with unstructured, collaborative data is allowing a much deeper insight into how companies really operate and how customers use a company's products to create their own value. Further, the application of the statistical techniques applied through Big Data leads to still deeper understanding of both your business and your customer's behavior. Through quantification, a company can quantify this value delivery, and thereby reduce the cost of delivering this value and driving profitability for its operations.

Quantification also supports the acceleration goals discussed in Chapter 14. If you set the goal of reducing the cycle time of all of your business processes by half every eighteen months, then you will need all of this process data to confirm that you are meeting this goal. Quantification is a process that many companies have already gone through, as it is a key aspect of deploying enterprise systems, such as Enterprise Resource Planning (ERP). However, in nearly all companies there remain dozens if not hundreds of additional business processes that are undefined and unmonitored from a data perspective. As long as these processes are not quantified, they will likely form bottlenecks in efforts to accelerate business. Quantifying these additional processes will facilitate business acceleration and will allow for fact-based decision making, which furthers a company's ability to respond to the ever-changing business climate.

The Analytic Executive: How Data Will Supplant Experience and Intuition

While there is much focus on the costs of managing massive amounts of data, there are also significant benefits to be gained by analyzing this information. The growing emphasis on data analysis stems from both the availability of massive amounts of data and the recent emergence of tools designed to digest it in large chunks. By 2020, the Big Data revolution will be over. Instead, there will be companies that have actively embraced data analytics as a core business process and there will be those companies that have elected to go out of business.

This may sound like a bold prediction, but I believe that the speed of business that we're experiencing means that today's opportunity becomes tomorrow's imperative. And tomorrow's imperative becomes the following day's obituary for those who don't act. Today's leading companies have already embraced data analysis as a core competency. If you're not one of them, then you're already in survival mode. In fact, in 2013, IBM predicted that its data analysis consulting business would exceed $20 billion in 2015; a doubling of the size of this business in only five years.[2]

Smart business people will be those who reprogram and reskill themselves for this analytic future. Data literacy will be a key determinant of business success in the coming decade, and thus will also be a determinant of career success. Whatever your background and whatever your skill set, your ability to understand and act upon data will determine your business' future success.

CHAPTER SUMMARY

1. If you do not have metrics and measurement in place for all of your business processes, implement such controls as soon as possible.

2. As outlined in Chapters 14 and 15, the metrics that you capture should allow you to measure how well you are applying the concepts of polarization and acceleration in your business.

3. Extend data metrics into nontraditional data channels, such as email, internal social media and collaboration platforms, and customer communication channels. Just as effective organizations maintain 360 degree reviews for their employees, you should implement 360 degree reviews of your business processes and your products and services.

16

quantification
big data, bigger results

AS STATED IN Chapter 9, any business process can be decomposed into a series of subprocesses, each of which generates some business outcome. Each of these outcomes can be treated as a business quanta, and any of these quanta that are commoditized or undifferentiated can and should be outsourced to maximize process efficiency. The key to making a business quanta outsourceable is to properly define all of its properties and characteristics. By doing so, you package the quanta and the process that created it, which makes it portable from an execution perspective.

I introduced quantification in the last chapter, and now I want to expand on that definition and discussion. In quantification, we develop all of the metrics that would characterize a business outcome from its required inputs, the expected outputs, and the tasks that convert the former into the latter. This isn't rocket science; it's basic systems engineering, and you might think that your company has already gone through this whole process. Ponder this: Has your company outsourced some or all of one of its business processes over the last 10 years? Chances are that it has. Next question: Have you heard any complaints about how that outsourcing worked out? Maybe there was poor service, maybe the service delivered didn't meet expectations, perhaps there were contractual issues where the outsourcee didn't produce your company's expected results, and so on. If your company has outsourced part of its business and doesn't have one or more of these complaints about the results, you're among the lucky minority.

I've seen a lot of outsourcing deals in my career, and the vast majority of them didn't work out as planned. Certainly, a range of factors has contributed to the issues involved. However, I'm pretty convinced that the most important factor determining the success or failure of outsourcing is proper definition of the expected outcomes, and definition of what it takes to achieve them. If there was a disagreement regarding what was delivered, it typically came down to poorly defined inputs, outputs, or the transformation from one to the other.

Defining Critical Metrics

The process of quantification boils down to the definition and tracking of metrics that drive each business process in your company. Nearly all companies have a set of core metrics that they follow to judge the ongoing health of the business. This is nothing new, and many managers are familiar with going through stacks and stacks of weekly or monthly reports trying to determine how well the business is doing. However, I have also found that the vast majority of metrics followed in companies focus on end results rather than on incremental results. This is a natural way of using metrics, since most organizations are strongly oriented toward their bottom line. Thus, the metrics usually tracked are those tied to resource utilization (costs) and sales (revenue).

Certainly these data points are critical to determining business health, as these are fundamental to the fiscal performance of the business. However, as businesses are forced to outsource more and more of their business processes and as their drive toward greater flexibility and efficiency of their incremental business outcomes, these high level metrics will lose a great deal of their importance. The reason is that metrics, such as costs, revenues, and profitability, are end results of business processes. They can tell you how well a set of processes have performed, but they reveal little regarding where there may be problems or opportunities within those same processes. Whether you are driving toward greater efficiency or greater flexibility, the need to increase your business velocity necessarily means that you need to look inside each of your business processes to find opportunities for improvement. This requires that your business metrics support the analysis of the business outcomes within your processes, so that you can find these potential areas of improvement. This much higher granularity of metrics will necessarily increase the amount of data that you're collecting and analyzing, but this is what will be required to accelerate your business through the discovery of an implementation of large numbers of outcome innovations. Again, whether you're a commodity business seeking greater efficiency or a value business seeking greater flexibility, the metrics that you collect and upon which you base your decisions will directly impact how successful you will be in remaining competitive.

Those metrics you choose to collect and act upon can vary greatly from industry to industry. However, it is important to remember the strategic guidance of Chapter 13, where the data that will be most valuable to you depends on your value proposition to your customers. If you're producing a commodity product, it's probably not necessary to tap into the full message feed from Twitter and Facebook to profile your customers. It would be imperative, however, to tap into your logistics provider, such as FedEx or UPS, and provide real-time tracking of customer orders. However, if you're a value-added provider, then how your customers feel about your product or service may be the most important information that you can gather, and so tapping into Twitter and Facebook may be a key driver of your process optimization efforts.

Implement Controls

Once all of the relevant metrics for a business process and its resulting outcomes have been defined, the next key is to define the controls for these metrics. This means setting boundaries for each of these metrics such that you can easily determine if your process is out of control or if your outcome is not meeting expectations. There is a whole body of work out there for determining such process controls, typically known as statistical process control (SPC). Many manufacturing companies have used SPC to find, analyze, and remove defects from their production processes, and premier manufacturers like General Electric, 3M, Ford, and Motorola have famously used SPC to vastly improve their operational processes.

This stuff has been around for over two decades, yet many companies still have not implemented these techniques for improving performance. This is particularly true of business processes that don't immediately lend themselves to quantifiable measurement. Examples of this might include HR processes like hiring or promoting and marketing processes like advertising or customer relationship management. Ironically, many of these same processes are the very ones that companies frequently outsource, ostensibly to improve their results.

Since most of these processes do not have metrics or controls defined for them, is it any wonder that when they are outsourced, the results are less than spectacular? The underlying problem is not that the process was outsourced or that the outsourcee cannot properly perform the process on your behalf. Rather, the problem is more likely that you haven't sufficiently defined the controls for the process. As such, you don't have a good way of knowing if the process is performing correctly or not and cannot take preventative measures when things start to go a little sideways.

If you buy into my predictions regarding "Everything as a Service," it should be apparent that these controls and metrics need to be in place if you are going to successfully leverage new resource markets. This will be even truer as we progress from outsourcing entire processes to outsourcing individual business outcomes, as discussed in Chapter 5.

Analyze, Optimize, and Automate

Once you have implemented metrics and controls, you are ready to begin analyzing the performance of your business processes to further optimize them. Such optimization will naturally include the outsourcing of some or all of the business outcomes used by each process, which you can now leverage because you have an adequate understanding of how those processes perform.

To achieve optimization, companies will need to become proficient at orchestration, that is, the coordination of all of these incremental business outcomes to produce the final outcomes that they expect. Assuming that a substantial number of your business outcomes within your processes will be outsourced in some manner, your ability to orchestrate the collection and aggregation of all of these outcomes and create your end product or service will be the final determinant of your business success. Successful companies in the near future will be those that can have each element or outcome used in producing their end product produced as efficiently as possible and having those results delivered back to the business in a just-in-time fashion. Speed will be the key, but to maintain control of highly outsourced business processes, orchestration will be the difference between success and failure.

Orchestration will be a challenge for companies following a commodity strategy, because as they grow ever more efficient, the profitability of each incremental unit that they sell may rely solely on a volume discount that they earned on one of their incremental outcomes. And, to earn this volume discount required that the company's prediction of future customer demand be nearly perfect all of the time.

Orchestration will be even more difficult for companies that follow a value-added strategy, as they will need to orchestrate their business outcomes so that they feed thousands, perhaps even millions, of markets of one. This is why it is critically important for value-delivery companies to identify those incremental, commodity business outcomes that are core to their products. Once these are identified, they can be made as efficiently as possible, perhaps even stockpiled, so that there is no delay in feeding the differentiating incremental outcomes that are the basis of customization to individual consumers.

An example might help make sense of this idea. Let's say that you're a famous wedding cake baker. You're known for your innovative cake designs, which are customized for every customer. Part of your value proposition is that no two cakes are ever the same. Generally, the bulk of the custom work involves designing unique decorating elements in frosting or fondant, which are then placed on cakes cut from standard shapes into those required for the given design.

For this business, the commodity, or the incremental outcome, are the cakes that are used as the basis for each custom cake. Consider the overall value chain here. The famous cake baker could easily charge a couple of thousand dollars for an innovative, custom-made cake. However, the actual cakes that are used to make up a finished cake cost perhaps 5 to 10 dollars each. They have trivial value compared to the end product, and yet they are absolutely critical to producing the end product.

As part of your business, you likely offer several different cake fillings, although there are only so many to choose from. And, since the cakes that you use all come from a few standard shapes (e.g., round, square, rectangular), the cakes that form the basis of each unique cake are indeed a commodity that, through optimization, might facilitate the speed and flexibility of your value-added business processes. How could you optimize your use of this commodity business input to maximize your revenue and profit?

If you offer 10 fillings for your cakes (vanilla, chocolate, etc.) and typically use five different shapes in creating your custom cakes, that's fifty possible variations for you to keep on hand. Since cakes can be prebaked and will keep for weeks or months if frozen, there is every reason to stock up on cakes, That way, they are readily at hand when a new custom cake is ordered. Further, it might even make sense to outsource the baking of the cakes to another baker, who would provide a steady stream of cakes which you would then use in your custom designs. Again, the cost of each cake is dramatically less than the value of one of your completed cakes, so maintaining a stock of them is not only affordable, it makes great business sense.

Now, as long as the cakes still taste good and none of this detracts from the buyer's experience, they can be truly be treated as a commodity incremental business outcome; you use these cakes to produce your final product, but how you obtain the cakes is largely irrelevant to the value of your end product. What's important is that they are available when you need them. The worst thing you could do is fail to deliver a customer order worth a few thousand dollars because you are missing one or more five dollar cakes. So again, it makes the most sense to keep some on hand, ready to go, or to outsource to another baker who can guarantee a just-in-time supply.

In this example, the focus of the business is a value-added, non-commodity end product. However, that end product necessarily relies on one or more components that are themselves commodities. To maximize profits in this business, the most important factor is to meet the need of every possible customer. In other words, never turn away a customer for lack of cakes. As such, the necessary step of quantification here is to establish and maintain a reliable supply of all fifty variations of cakes that you might use so that you never have to turn away a customer. Certainly, there may be some waste from this approach, and you might not use some of the cakes that you have on hand before they go stale. However, you can lose two hundred such cakes for the revenue generated by a single sale, so the business case strongly supports keeping stock on hand.

However, you may be in a pure commodity business, that is, one in which there is substantial competition and little differentiation. Here, maximizing the cost efficiency of every step of your business processes is critical to overall success, as with the baker who supplies the basic cakes in the example above. This is particularly true in today's business environment, where the Internet provides customers with extreme market transparency and nearly perfect competition.

Quantification is not a new concept to modern businesses. However, the scale and scope of the metrics and controls that companies must deploy and use is going to grow dramatically over the next 10 years. As business processes continue to accelerate, business volumes continue to grow, and more and more business activity is outsourced into outcome markets, businesses will rely even more on automated metrics and controls to properly orchestrate all of these activities and ensure that the business performs according to expectations. All of this orchestration will necessarily involve the creation and analysis of vastly greater quantities of operational data. Furthering the data crush with which companies must contend.

CHAPTER SUMMARY

1. Defining critical metrics is the key initial step in quantifying your business. All aspects of the inputs and outputs of each business process should be defined, so that the success or failure of the process execution may be accurately measured.

2. Once critical operational data is defined, controls should be established so that process performance can be tracked and improved through ongoing optimization or outsourcing efforts.

3. As process performance improves through metrics and controls, businesses should seek to further improve their performance through statistical analysis, exception handling, and predictive monitoring. One key goal of this effort should be to accelerate the cycle time of all business processes, seeking to cut cycle times in half every 12 to 18 months.

17

gamify
getting what you pay for

AS ESTABLISHED IN Chapter 4, digital entertainment has become a driving cultural force. Indeed, making the user experience engaging and entertaining is a critical element of business success online. The vast majority of people are now very comfortable with following a set of tasks, potentially ones that get increasingly complex as you go through them, and then receiving a score once the tasks are completed. Even better are those scenarios where the participant/player receives some sort of recognition or reward based on how well they perform the tasks versus some standard or versus the performance of others. The process of making work seem like play, or "gamification," will be a critical driver of digital strategy over the next 10 years.

In simple terms, gamification is the application of game or sports concepts (e.g., competition, points, awards), to business processes. Using the ever-popular game Tetris as an example, game players are given a task (building completed rows of boxes from shapes that fall down the computer screen) and, as they complete this repetitive task, they build up their score. As the game progresses, it gets more and more difficult (in Tetris, the pieces fall faster and faster as the player advances), and therefore more and more challenging to the players. The game ends once the difficulty of the game exceeds a player's ability to keep up, thereby challenging the player to improve skills and achieve a higher score.

If we apply gamification to a business process, we would apply these very same rules to attempt to achieve better outcomes. Following the guidance on the need for business acceleration from Chapter 14, let's say that we wish to double the throughput of a given business process using the same resources. If we put in place a scoring mechanism, allow for the process participant to follow that score, and then give the participant the goal of doubling the throughput, you might be surprised how much that participant may be able to improve performance—just because of this positive feedback mechanism. When gamification concepts are applied to rudimentary or even boring tasks, users are more motivated to complete them and to improve performance. Indeed, if you give such process participants goals that really stretch their abilities, you may find that they start to think out of the box and come up with new ways of performing their tasks that will lead to better scores. Gamification can therefore stimulate innovation—all at little or no cost to the company.

As improbable as this may seem, cutting-edge companies such as Home Depot, Amazon, and Walmart have already adopted this approach to business and have seen tremendous returns on their investments. What is interesting about gamification is that it works equally well in motivating customers or employees; the incentive effect is the same in either case. Thus, if you properly apply gamification to your business, you may not only improve the productivity of your employees, you might actually be able to guide the behavior of your customers and extract more value from them.

If you have played the Monopoly game at McDonalds over the last twenty-five years, then you have been a gamified customer. McDonalds has been remarkably successful with this game, using monopoly pieces to drive customer buying behavior. If you've ever wondered why you get Monopoly game pieces from McDonalds only when you buy certain menu items, it is because those particular products are the company's most profitable. McDonalds uses the popularity of the game to drive up sales of those products that generate the most profit. The incremental sales of these items more than makes up for the cost of the prizes that McDonalds awards its customers.

Indeed, many of the prizes that people get are for free menu items. Those items are not ones that you would typically purchase on their own (how many people buy just a small order of French fries or a medium drink), so the prize that is awarded typically drives further sales of other items. While this example doesn't fully leverage the power of online commerce or of data analysis, it should certainly support the thesis that gamification can have a powerful effect upon consumer behavior.

Getting Your Game On

Perhaps the easiest place to start gamifying your business is to implement scoring mechanisms in the collaboration tools that your company has hopefully deployed by now. Although not the only collaboration platform out there, Microsoft's SharePoint product is in use by over 70 percent of all of the companies in the world, some-times whether they know it or not! SharePoint is a software product that allows users to publish and share documents, start online con-versations on a range of topics, give teams a virtual team room where they can collaborate, and manage many other productivity features. These tools tend to polarize their intended audience. People either love it or can't be bothered with it. However, for those business teams that have bought into the SharePoint idiom, this tool rapidly becomes the critical nexus of how their team members interact with each other.

With nearly all of these functions, Microsoft has enabled Share-Point to support scoring. If someone reads a post on SharePoint, that person can actually rate that post based on its business value, quality of content, relevancy, and so on. In other words, SharePoint is gamified. It supports the ranking of documents and posts, it allows people to "like" something SharePoint manages, and it starts to build up data related to the apparent quality of the work products that people place within SharePoint. What this means is that it is en-tirely likely that your business is already gamifying at least some of its content and processes, even if your management hasn't actively chosen to do so.

This will also be the case if your company is maintaining a pres-ence on social platforms like Facebook, where people again can "like" materials that you post to the site, and thereby start a scoring mechanism that you can track. The key to starting to gain value from gamification is simple—take it seriously and have high expec-tations. Although we're talking about making work more fun, the process itself is scientific and needs to be managed very closely to ensure that you're achieving the results that you hoped for. When-ever you come up against organizational resistance to gamification, and you will, remind those naysayers of the size of the gaming market and the fact that game playing is deeply ingrained in the psyche of most employees and customers. Game playing has become a major element in the advanced training provided by today's military, so one would hope that it would be good enough for business processes that don't involve military weapons.

Recognize and Reward

When people start to gamify work processes and outcomes, most experience an interesting phenomenon. Some people are turned off by gamification; they don't like having their work products "scored" by their peers or customers. Alternatively, some people love this feedback and, indeed, they have probably felt starved for such feedback at work for some time. Do you want to take a guess as to which population of users should be the ambassadors of your gamification efforts? Here's a hint: choose the latter group!

Starting with your collaboration platforms and social media sites, begin setting up scoring opportunities and establish a rewards system based on these scores. The rewards do not need to be substantial, but they do need to be recognized and publicized; the more the better. In this way, you will begin to reinforce the behavior of the potential participants, whether they are employees, customers, or both. As some proportion of the user community starts to drive up its scores, be sure to celebrate those achievements, and then create further challenges.

Fairly rapidly, you will develop a community of users who are highly motivated to create work products for your business and are also motivated to make these work products as high quality as possible. If these products come from some of your existing employees, great. You just identified some of your most valuable people. If they come from customers, it is likely that you will find that these people are among your most profitable customers, in addition to working for you for free.

Adapt and Expand

Current estimates are that the commercial market for mobile goods and services should exceed $1 trillion by 2016.[1] It could easily be two to three times that size by 2020. Regardless of your industry, your size, or your location, if you're not running at least half of your business through mobile sources by 2020, you're likely in trouble. Further, I don't make a distinction between external business (your interactions with your own customers) and internal business (interactions within your organization or across the vendors in your value chain). Again, at least half of your business should be flowing through the mobile channel by then; hopefully, a great deal more.

As of 2013, the number one activity that users performed on their smartphones was game playing[2]; they did this more than talking or web surfing. If you're planning on using gamification to improve your business and you want to partake in the explosive growth of mobility over the next 10 years, then you're in luck. Companies that figure out how to gamify their customers' mobile experience are likely to win the customer attention battle predicted in Chapter 10. Because of this, I believe that successful companies will embrace gamification as a key to their productivity growth over the next decade.

If you haven't done this before (and if you haven't, shame on you!), log into YouTube and search for videos that are about the products or services your company provides. If you don't find multiple customer-generated videos on your product or service I'd be surprised—and you should probably be worried. With so much content dumped into YouTube every day, you should hope that at least some customer is talking about your company and what you mean to them. So, if your products or services aren't even mentioned on YouTube, you have a much bigger problem.

Now, let's say that you did search on something your company sells and one or more of the results turned out to be negative. Congratulations! You just found a phenomenal marketing opportunity, but you must act quickly and decisively. If someone has complained online about what you've done or haven't done, then reward them for putting forth the effort to speak about it. Simply engaging that person for their negative commentary is likely to soften the tone. If, then, you give the person a reward for identifying a shortcoming in your business, you may very well turn around their negative view. Since this person has already identified himself or herself as someone who will use the Internet as a forum for sharing opinions, that person is likely to report to the world how great you subsequently treated them. This is very rudimentary gamification, but this is something that you could readily put into place today, as many companies already have.

As a process, gamification will introduce a range of new data collection and management points to your business. You'll need to provide users with the ability to provide feedback, you'll need to maintain the score that different content elements and/or users establish, and you'll need to implement and manage mechanisms for rewarding high performers. There are many tools that either support this sort of functionality or that allow you to manage gamification of other software tools.

While supporting this functionality will require additional effort, time, and money on the part of your business, the benefits should clearly outweigh these incremental costs. Simply identifying those people in your organization who are clearly adding value in a quantifiable way should be worth the effort required to deploy and support gamification. Similarly, setting up your various online channels to be gamified will certainly add cost to your operations. However, the customer data that you can collect and the content that you might harvest from your customers should more than make up for these incremental costs.

Gamification is yet another method of enhancing customer engagement, on the path toward customer intimacy. It is a method for plugging into the participation imperative discussed in Chapter 2. Whether playing games, contributing to blogs, or submitting home videos, customers these days want to participate in their life activities. And, if you provide a platform where these same people can receive positive feedback for their contributions, you will bring them back to your platforms like bees to honey. The attraction of audience feedback can be addictive, and it is this effect that you're trying to encourage through gamification.

If you look around today, you'll find that many large and successful businesses have already embraced gamification. These companies are harvesting additional value from both employees and customers by properly motivating them through gaming concepts like scoring, levels, advancement, and rewards. There is no reason that work has to be dull, boring, and potentially even dehumanizing. Rather, by applying gamification principles, it is possible to get people to enjoy contributing value to your business. Remember that the incremental cost of this added value is negligible. Gamification will almost certainly add to the productivity of human capital and can also facilitate the advancement of your business processes. This is becoming an imperative due to the changes described in Parts One and Two.

CHAPTER SUMMARY

1. If you haven't already done so, begin gamifying your internal collaboration platforms as soon as possible. Start to identify those employees who thrive in this environment and encourage their growing contributions to your business.

2. Also, gamify your online customer interactions; on your company website, blogs, and Social Media accounts. Here too, start to identify those customers who engage with you through these gamified interactions, and seek to create a population of customers who begin to create business value through their gamified interactions with your business.

3. Set up appropriate analytical capability so that you can begin to measure and make sense of the results of your gamification efforts, particularly those focused on customer interaction. Your goal should be to determine the profitability that you derive from customers who participate in your gamification efforts, and then to grow that profitability as quickly as possible.

4. Set a strategy and a budget to monetize your gamification efforts. Use the combination of recognition and cold, hard cash to drive adoption of your gamified platforms, further improving both revenues and profits.

18

crowdsource
putting your audience to work

CHAPTER 10 reviewed how the wealth of corporate operational data allows companies to create and then outsource an ever-
expanding proportion of their business processes. This phenomenon
is creating a new generation of business utilities—processes where
inputs and outputs are managed by outside organizations. These
companies have optimized their processes to produce predictable
results at minimal cost.

Examples of such companies include Paychex and Ambrose HR,
companies that specialize in delivering a practical, reliable business
provide information results. The goal of these organizations is to
provide an information service that is as invisible as electric or water
service in our homes. They also seek to do so at a cost far below that
of a company attempting to produce the same result internally. In-

deed, most venture capitalists today will not even consider funding a startup company without fully leveraged utility services as part of their operating model.

These providers achieve their outstanding results because they can digest and use the vast quantities of data at their disposal. As they sign up more and more customers, they continue to gain deeper and more meaningful insights into how to get results at maximum efficiency and lowest cost. These efficiencies make these providers much better at delivering incremental business outcomes than their customers, which explains why process outsourcing grew into a one trillion dollar industry by 2013.[1] The bulk of outsourced work is presently process-centric. That is, entire business processes, such as human resources, customer relationship management, and payroll are outsourced in their entirety. However, this trend is likely to change over the coming 10 years, as more and more markets develop for the outsourcing of subprocesses, rather than entire processes.

The driver for this further delineation of the outsourcing world will be the need for both greater efficiency and greater flexibility of organizations. As discussed in Chapter 13, changes to the competitive landscape will force companies to become either more efficient or more flexible in their operations; or perhaps both. Since the vast majority of Fortune 1000 companies have already embraced outsourcing to some degree, more pressure will be placed upon outsourcees to provide these improvements in their services.

In order to be either more efficient or more flexible, outsourcees will themselves begin to outsource parts of their business operations to smaller, more focused organizations that specialize in producing certain smaller business outcomes that are critical to higher level business processes. For example, Paychex is a leading provider of payroll processing services as an outsourcee to other companies. In turn, Paychex may find it to be more efficient to outsource its own needs for printing services to another third-party provider rather than perform this task in-house. To maximize the efficiency with which it receives this outsourced service, Paychex may actually create and maintain a marketplace for printing services, where multiple printing vendors can compete with one another to fulfill the printing work that Paychex is looking to outsource. Such a marketplace would maximize the value to Paychex, which could then pass on this savings to its customers by becoming more competitive in its own marketplace, and so on.

I expect that the forces of socialfication, contextification, and quantafication, along with the availability of a global workforce, will make such micromarketplaces common through the 2010s, which should lead to the widespread adoption of crowdsourcing. By crowdsourcing, I mean the trend toward outsourcing smaller and smaller pieces of work, or business quanta, as presented in Chapter 9, to groups or crowds of potential providers. As these marketplaces for labor and business outcomes grow, they will drive both greater efficiency and greater flexibility into the business processes of outsourcing companies, which is exactly what these companies will require to remain competitive as discussed in Chapter 13. Additionally, most, if not all, of these crowds of new outcome providers will be cloud based due to their own need to be as efficient and flexible as possible. Thus, crowdsourcing will quickly evolve into cloudsourcing, where the company performing the original outsourcing will lose some degree of control over exactly what company delivers the work product and how it is delivered, but will accept these losses of control due to the benefits that cloudsourcing brings.

Crowdsourcing and even cloudsourcing are not new. They have been around as long as the Internet. Perhaps the best example of crowdsourcing at work is the Linux operating system. Linux started out as a project to develop an operating system that was freeware; anyone could use it without having to pay some company for a license. Over many years, thousands of people contributed their time, effort, and expertise to the development of an operating system that was the equal of, if not significantly better than, other operating systems, such as Unix or Microsoft's Windows.

Over time, Linux was commercialized by several companies, such as RedHat, that leveraged the efficiencies inherent in the design of Linux to capture market share from competing systems. As a result, Linux has become a technology standard for most Fortune 1000 companies, again, proving the success of the crowdsourcing model when properly applied.

As its name implies, crowdsourcing will involve large numbers of players participating in large numbers of transactions. This will naturally lead to the generation of vast quantities of data. Leveraging this data will allow companies to further refine and optimize the outputs created by crowdsourced markets and will allow the company to score different providers in a gamified manner. Again, crowdsourcing will be an end-product of companies adaptation to the six changes outlined in Part Two, as well as implementing the other five approaches outlined in Part Three.

Design for Merchantability

Design for merchantability is the process by which you make your business more outsourcing friendly. By applying the principles of gamification, quantafication, quantification, and the others discussed, you can set up your organization to benefit greatly from the new markets for labor and business outcomes that will be created during the coming decade. Leveraging these markets in the proper way will be critical to every company's competitiveness in the emerging social economy. So, aligning your business to participate in these markets will determine your future success.

As discussed, quantafication will allow you to create business processes that are packaged to facilitate outsourcing, where appropriate. Quantification will provide critical metrics and controls that will ensure that outsourced business outcomes meet or exceed your customers' expectations. Socialfication will ensure that you're engaged with audiences of both customers and potential service providers, so that you can source your business outcomes appropriately. Finally, gamification will ensure that working with your organization is "fun" and provides appropriate psychological and financial rewards to those who produce the best results for you. By this point, I hope it is obvious that all of these forces are deeply interdependent and that your company's response to these forces and adaptation to them must take these interdependencies into consideration.

Crowdsourcing Imperative: Encouraging Markets and Attracting Resources

In order to properly leverage this trend toward greater efficiency and flexibility, both outsourcers and first-generation outsourcees will have to create marketplaces for business outcomes. These marketplaces will start slowly, but will rapidly grow at the pace we see as normal these days—in other words, explosively. The reasons for this should be clear. A huge population of people are readily accessible through a variety of social platforms. Many of them are looking for work and also have skills that will become increasingly hard to come by because of the aging of the Baby Boomer generation. Further, the ever-increasing demand by outsourcers for greater efficiency and flexibility will reinforce the need for these marketplaces, even as advances in cloud computing and quantafication make it easier for these organizations to pick up the workload from outsourcing companies. As such, all companies, whether outsourcers or outsourcees, should be encouraging the development of these marketplaces, both for short-term gains and long-term survival.

Another factor contributing to the growth of crowdsourcing and eventually cloudsourcing will be the widespread adoption of gamification. Once gamification takes hold of core business processes, it is not too large a step to monetize them. This necessarily leads to the creation of an outcome market, which should in itself be one of your business goals. As mentioned, one side effect of gamification is that it introduces an entirely new source of labor to organizations that will embrace it. Given that the globally connected audience exceeds six billion and that this audience is constantly in search of novelty, companies that can add "fun and games" to corporate tasks will find a huge pool of available labor. This is a market willing and able to perform tasks for free, or nearly so, working instead for points, virtual gifts, and other psychological rewards.

Anyone who doubts that this market is a serious should look at innovators, such as Sephora, Verizon, or Home Depot—companies that not only deeply engage their customers, but actually put them to work. Their social media presence has morphed into "content factories"—places where product reviews, testimonials, training, and marketing materials are created for free by customers. In turn, through their contributions, these people become more engaged and thus far more profitable to their sponsoring companies.

For example, Home Depot's website offers a wide range of content related to both its product offerings and how you might use them to complete a project. While some of this content is created by Home Depot employees, a large quantity is generated by customers. Home Depot encourages customers with unique experiences, ideas, and advice to contribute to the website, enriching what is available to others. This costs next to nothing for Home Depot to support and yet adds tremendous value for customers looking for such guidance on how to perform specific tasks.

Putting Customers to Work: Feeding Egos, Filling Coffers

So, how do you start tapping into this resource ocean? How do you engage with customers so that they want to work for you? To achieve this, you need to mix a healthy portion of socialfication, cloudification, and gamification, which together form a potent recipe for the creation of new, compelling, and nearly free content which you can then leverage across your entire business.

By 2013, many examples of this existed. A good one can be found in Home Depot's online presence. As part of its efforts to help do-it-yourselfers, who are a substantial proportion of its customer base, Home Depot has created a wealth of user-oriented content on their website. From how-to videos to question and answer guides, Home Depot has created a rich customer experience that reinforces its brand identity. This material draws in customers and gets them engaged with Home Depot as a solutions vendor, rather than just as a home products store.

In the content presented on Home Depot.com, there is a large blog area where customers can post relevant content for others to read. This material can vary from product reviews to guidance on how to perform certain home improvement tasks to various secrets and best practices for a range of tasks around the house. The materials provided are typically posted by customers or other nonemployees of the company, although Home Depot certainly maintains a degree of control over what gets posted. Other customers can read these posts and rank them as to their usefulness, which is a direct example of gamification.

It wouldn't be a tremendous stretch for Home Depot to reach out to those people who have provided particularly useful posts to these blogs and compensate them for adding to their posts. These people could be paid to answer customer questions or issues or to add to the body of content they've placed on the blogs. The more and better the content that they contribute, the more compensation they can potentially earn. In this way, Home Depot could try the waters of cloudsourcing in a relatively benign area of its business. From these early lessons, potentially more and more business outcomes could be served by outcome marketplaces, and Home Depot could begin to fully leverage crowdsourcing as a source of labor and expertise.

There are two potential areas of concern in following this approach. First, Home Depot must ensure that those who are providing content know what they are talking about and that they are people with whom Home Depot would want to be associated. Second, Home Depot would want to ensure that it is protected from potential risks created by the work product of those with whom they engage. If these issues are not adequately resolved, companies may be worried about engaging outside workers in this manner, and rightfully so.

Both of these issues will be addressed by marketplace sponsors, as they develop. Indeed, this is one of the main value propositions of formalized marketplaces for crowdsourced resources: validation and verification of those who wish to participate in the marketplace as both suppliers and customers.

Crowdsourcing: Attacking Work in Bite-Sized Nuggets

During the next decade, today's mechanisms for the social creation of content and conversation should morph into something greater: actual work product. Users who score particularly high in the gamified social sites that companies foster will become outside consultants of a sort. Their ongoing contribution of useful content will earn them greater and greater recognition by companies and their customers. This usefulness will become so sufficient that companies will be strongly motivated to sponsor these people formally; turning them into paid consultants, as with Jared Fogle and Subway.

These people may take on an ever-greater range of topics for their sponsoring companies, and their roles will become one of pseudoemployee. Further, their contributions and payouts will also look more and more like those of traditional contractors or consultants. For example, a person with high rank on a company's social site might evaluate new products today. In five years, that same person may be paid to attend panels for new product definition and development, and compensation for their time will morph from "points" and discounts into actual dollars. These changes will take place subtly, not necessarily by design. Once a company has identified various social superstars, it will simply make sense to make further productive use of their input and to reward their greater contributions in kind.

This effect will grow, along with the general trend toward outsourcing, so that more and more of a company's functions will be performed by outside players. Fold in the explosive growth of micro-markets and the near future businesses will have to adapt to the rapid growth of crowdsourcing.

Crowdsourcing will be the evolution of business so that internal processes are broken down into their basic elements; each process defined as a series of steps, each with well-defined inputs and well-defined outcomes (quantafication). Since each step of the business process is quantized, each step can be individually outsourced to whomever is both qualified to generate the business outcome and offers the lowest bid to perform the work. Thus, rather than outsourcing entire business processes to a single vendor in the hope that it can properly manage all of the inputs and outputs, companies will manage the process themselves, outsourcing each element to a collection of delivery organizations and individuals. By this mechanism, companies can retain control of both their processes and their critical business data and still receive the benefits of outside expertise and price competition.

The move to cloudsourcing will be the final step in this transformation of outsourcing, in which outsourcers give up a degree of control over how their outsourced processes work to gain the benefits of greater efficiency and flexibility. Outsourcers will put their work requirements into cloud-based marketplaces where large numbers of vendors, both individuals and groups, will compete for this work. Those who win the competition will produce the business outcomes according to the requirements of the outsourcer, but without the outsourcer specifying how those outcomes are produced. This caveat is critical to the growth of cloudsourcing, as it will allow outsourcees to focus upon innovating their own processes to become more competitive in their niche space.

Initially, outsourcers will be pretty uncomfortable with giving up this degree of process control and oversight. Indeed, they may believe that they cannot do so, from either a liability or regulatory perspective. However, I believe that these markets will grow and adapt even to these restrictive requirements. I've spoken with a large number of business executives who are actively looking for ways in which they could outsource some of their regulatory requirements to one or more third parties. Interestingly, the challenges of regulatory compliance and risk management may actually drive customers toward cloudsourcing. There are relatively few experts in dealing with these issues, making it difficult for many companies to hire the necessary expertise. Through cloudsourcing, rare and hard-to-obtain experts may be leveraged across a wide range of customers. This will prove particularly useful to small and mid-sized companies in highly regulated industries such as healthcare or finance.

Through cloudsourcing, entire new industries will emerge over the coming decade, many populated by startup companies, others populated by individuals with special skills or experience, and all of them driving forward the dual business goals of flexibility and efficiency. These marketplaces and the businesses that participate in them will be both contributors to and beneficiaries of the gargantuan explosion of information that we will witness over the next 10 years—a crush of data the size of which we can only guess.

CHAPTER SUMMARY

1. Implement cloudification, quantification, and quantafication to make your business crowdsourceable.

2. Seek to identify those people in your organization who are strong at organizing and orchestrating business processes. These people will be key to managing operational effectiveness once more of your value chain is placed in cloud markets.

3. As outcome markets appear, begin leveraging their productivity and efficiency. Initially, participate in small increments, ensuring that your organization can operate in a hybrid outcome model.

4. Use gamification to enhance crowdsourcing outcomes. Try to establish market "buzz" around the benefits of working with your organization and reward those who produce results beyond merely delivering your expected outcomes.

summary
a few days in life, circa 2020

AT THIS POINT, we have covered a great deal of territory. From the market forces that are driving massive data growth throughout our society to the responses that companies will need to formulate to remain relevant in our rapidly changing world, this book was intended to stimulate your imagination and hopefully help you set a course for your own work.

I've created five scenarios for the year 2020 that present what the near future might look like given the trends discussed in these chapters. In each case, I've reviewed the present trends in technology development and evolution, as well as the social trends that these advancements are enabling. In each example, I have shown how all of these trends and responses will intertwine and generate new opportunities and new challenges for companies that seek to remain competitive in the future that I am envisioning.

Some of my predictions may be a bit off, but I suspect not. Indeed, with how fast things are changing, some of them may actually fall quite a bit short of our reality in 2020. Still, my goal is to show the environment in which companies will have to operate as a result of the data crush that will continue to accelerate. Through these scenarios, companies will better understand the need to implement an integrated and comprehensive strategy to grow up the maturity models presented in Part Two.

Scenario 1: A Quick Trip to Vegas, Friday, April 10, 2020

Early on a Friday, Bill, a mortgage broker living and working in Orange County, California, receives an email offer from Epiphany, the newest and coolest hotel and casino on the Las Vegas strip. This coming weekend, Epiphany is hosting the annual mountain biking convention with over 50,000 people expected to attend. According to the email, Bill can stay two nights at Epiphany for a 75 percent discount and will also receive a 75 percent discount on the convention attendance fee. Further, he will receive a $50 coupon good for the purchase of a mountain bike during the convention, if he finds one that he likes.

Bill checks his calendar and realizes that he has the time to make it to Vegas that evening, stay through the weekend, and be back late on Sunday. It'll be a four-hour drive each way, but it sounds like fun, and he's been looking to buy a new mountain bike for a while now. He quickly posts on Facebook that he's going to Vegas that night and continues the rest of his work day.

After work, Bill quickly stops by his apartment, loads a duffle bag with toiletries and clothes for a couple of days, and then jumps into his car. He heads north toward Vegas, and about halfway through the trip his car instructs him to pull off of the road at Ted's Gas and Go. Bill lets the pump scan the screen of his iPhone 12 and starts pumping gas; at $7.35 a gallon, it's a great price! His phone points out the Starbucks across the street, and Bill drives over to pick up a drink with the coupon on his phone.

Bill orders a nonfat, organic-dairy, fair-trade, green-energy-brewed grande latté; coincidentally on sale for the same price as the gas he just bought: $7.35. He hops back in his car and continues on to Vegas, arriving late on Friday.

In the morning, he meets for breakfast with his friend Tom, who has two new acquaintances Kathy and Jason. It turns out that all four have been looking to buy a new mountain bike, and they all received discounts for staying at the Epiphany and attending the convention. They compare notes over breakfast on favorite biking spots, sharing the geolocations with each other before they finish their breakfast and head to the conference.

As Bill walks into the convention center he notices that a conference app autoloaded on his phone, giving him directions around the convention, schedules for events and demonstrations, and instructions for a scavenger hunt where prizes will be awarded to whomever finds all of the items on the list. He can already see that other people have found 12 of the 25 items on the list, so he decides to pass on the scavenger hunt. Instead, he heads over to the display area for Biketilla the Hun brand bikes . . . the brand he was looking to buy a few weeks ago while shopping online.

With the coupon that he received from the Epiphany, Bill finds that he can buy a Savage 250 model bike from Biketilla for almost $300 less than he would have paid at the local bike shop. So he buys the bike with his credit card, arranging for delivery in the following week. Because he purchased the bike at the show, he receives a 30 percent discount on dinner at any of Epiphany's dozen restaurants. He browses through the rest of the show, looking at other accessories that might be of interest. Then, he leaves the show and tries to decide where to eat dinner.

Around 4 PM, Bill gets an email inviting him to a dinner get-together at Squishy Sushi, the flagship restaurant at Epiphany. He shows up around 6 PM and finds that he'll be sharing dinner with other buyers and owners of Savage 250s, along with the Savage 250 product manager from Biketilla the Hun, Inc. Dinner is very entertaining, with the owners of the Savage sharing stories of how and where they use their bikes, and the new owners looking forward to having similar experiences themselves. Bill heads back to his room with even greater anticipation of receiving his new bike and with 15 new Facebook "friends" as a result of the dinner.

The next day, Bill packs up and clicks "checkout" on the Epiphany app that he downloaded when he arrived. When he gets to the lobby, his car is waiting for him at checkout, his bill has been emailed to him, and his key automatically deactivated. On the drive back home, he gets another email offer from the Starbucks he visited on the way there, but he didn't really feel like coffee right now. He arrived home late that Sunday night, unpacked, and went to sleep anticipating the rides that he would soon take on his new Savage 250 mountain bike.

Behind the Scenes

Throughout this scenario, Bill takes advantage of offers and deals that seem to appear out of thin air at just the right time. However, let's take a look at what transpired behind the scenes to make all of this possible.

DISCOUNT AT THE EPIPHANY

Over the prior several weeks, Bill had been researching several different models of mountain bike, trying to decide which he wanted to buy. He visited Biketilla the Hun's website several times and had mentioned the savage 250 as his preferred model on his Facebook site and a couple of twitter posts. Biketilla found these posts in its market research (*Big Data analysis of social media feeds*) and validated Bill as a likely customer based upon his profile online (*steady job with a good income, spends time and money on his hobbies, thus has disposable income*) and then targeted him for the Vegas visit promotion.

The discount provided by Epiphany was partly paid for by the hotel, partly paid by the convention promoters, and partly paid by Biketilla (a shared proximate investment by all parties). The promotional invitation went out the day before the convention as the convention was underbooked and the promoter was looking to fill up those rooms that they had reserved in advance.

BUYING GAS AT TED'S

Bill has an app, GasFinder, that constantly looks for deals on gas for drivers. GasFinder aggregates drivers in need of gasoline along a given corridor and aggregates their purchasing power in a reverse-Groupon auction (*appification, quantafication, and cloudification*). Gas stations along the corridor are allowed to bid on groups of buyers and provide a discount based on the group purchase. GasFinder receives a percentage of the discount as a small payment from each buyer in the transaction (*crowdsourcing, cloudification, and quantafication*). Further, Bill has a "green-friendly" stipulation on his AppNanny concierge app, which meant that he would only buy from a gas station that sold gas that was at least 20 percent renewable biofuel. While Jill's Gas and Jerky was $.15 cheaper per gallon, Jill's gas was only 15 percent biofuel, so they lost out on the reverse auction.

DISCOUNT AT STARBUCKS

Ted's had signed up for a proximate market with the Starbucks across the street. Thus, when Bill stopped at Ted's to fill up, the Starbucks was notified of a potential customer in Bill (*contextification*). Starbucks contacted and read Bill's AppNanny profile and knew that Bill was into organic foods, was currently on a diet, and was concerned about fair trade and green economics. So, it sent him a deal on the latté that best matched his profile (*contextification*).

When Bill bought the coffee, Ted's received a micropayment of $.25 for the referral (*quantafication and crowdsourcing*). Also, the caffeine load of the grande latté was registered with Bill's personal health app and became part of his health profile that was downloaded to his doctor and his health insurance provider on his next checkup.

Further, because Epiphany registered Bill's anticipated trip with AppNanny, Epiphany received a $.10 micropayment from both Ted's and Starbucks, as part of the proximate market supported by AppNanny (*quantafication and crowdsourcing*).

SATURDAY BREAKFAST

Bill's breakfast was automatically arranged by AppNanny, which knew that Tom was attending the convention. It also knew that Kathy and Jason had both signed up for the same promotional offer from Epiphany and thus, the group would likely have a great deal in common (*contextification*). Epiphany made a proximate payment to Biketilla, based upon the revenue earned from the breakfast that they all purchased (*crowdsourcing and quantafication*).

ATTENDING THE CONFERENCE

Epiphany knew that Bill was at the hotel to attend the conference, so with permission from AppNanny, Epiphany autoloaded the Mountain Bike Conference App on Bill's phone and made sure that Bill was aware of the location of Biketilla's show booth (*appification*). As Bill approached the Biketilla booth, a sales representative was notified of his approach, that he was a prequalified potential customer, and of his preference for a Savage 250 based upon his Facebook and Twitter traffic (*contextification*). The sales person was preauthorized to offer Bill the special discount on top of the $50 coupon provided by Epiphany and also knew of the location of the Savage 250 in Bill's preferred color closest to Bill's home. When Bill purchased the bike, proximate payments were made to the conference organizers and Epiphany for their contribution to the sale (*crowdsourcing and cloudification*).

DINNER AT SQUISHY'S

The dinner at Squishy's was planned and sponsored by Biketilla to strengthen the sense of community with its new customers. Epiphany provided the discount to ensure that the

Biketilla guests all ate at one of Epiphany's restaurants, and Biketilla made a proximate payment to Epiphany for ensuring that Biketilla's new customers attended the session (*crowdsourcing and cloudification*). Biketilla arranged for three to four existing customers to attend the conference at a deep discount, as part of their reward for their extensive participation on Biketilla's social media sites and online blogs (*gamification*). By bringing these new customers together with existing online "fans," Biketilla ensured the ongoing strengthening of its brand and online communities.

EPIPHANY CHECKOUT

When Bill hit "checkout" on his Epiphany app, he kicked off a number of workflows that ensured his checkout would be seamless. Housekeeping was notified that his room was now available for cleanup, the valet was notified to bring his car around, his account was automatically closed, his credit card was charged, and a flurry of micropayments were made with all of the influencers of the entire transaction, including the payment to AppNanny, for orchestrating the entire series of events (*contextification, cloudification, and crowdsourcing*).

Scenario 2: A New Year's Resolution, Wednesday, January 1, 2020

Tammy, a 24-year-old, works for a Fortune 500 company as an administrative assistant. She decides that her new year's resolution for 2020 will be to lose 15 pounds. She's relatively healthy but would love to drop a dress size in the coming five months as her best friend from college is getting married in May and Tammy is the maid of honor.

To help her, Tammy downloaded the Diet Defcon app for her smartphone, completed the initiation form, providing her present weight, her goal weight and dress size, diet start and end dates, and so on. She then synchronized the app with her personal health record app from the U.S. Department of Health, giving Diet Defcon access to some of the information on her medical records, such as body mass index (BMI). She gave Diet Defcon access to her Facebook and Twitter accounts, so that it could profile her likes and dislikes. Then, Diet Defcon constructed a diet scenario for her.

The following morning, her smartphone woke her up at 6:30 AM and gave her the choice of either jogging for a mile or walking for three miles. Feeling particularly motivated, Tammy decided to try the one-mile run. Diet Defcon suggested a running route around her neighborhood that she agreed to follow. She turned on the music player on her phone, which started to play some of her favorite up-tempo songs to help her keep up her running pace. As she hadn't gone for a run in quite a while, she grew tired around ¾ of a mile into the run, but her phone began to give her a pep talk over the music that was playing, encouraging her to finish the day's run and reminding her of the wedding coming up in just 99 days.

After she got back to her apartment, Defcon suggested a light breakfast, keeping track of her calorie intake by following the menu provided. After eating, she showered and got ready for work, posting to Facebook that she was following the diet to the letter, so far.

Later that day, Defcon notified her that 35 of her friends had agreed to sponsor her diet, each pledging $1 for every pound that she lost. Later that day, she received a shopping list from Defcon, which included coupons providing large discounts on the foods that Defcon wanted her to eat. After work she stopped at the store, picked up her food items, and headed home.

The next morning, she stepped on her scale, and saw that her weight hadn't changed. Defcon registered her weight and gave her the option of a 1.25-mile run or a 4-mile walk. Feeling energized, Tammy elected to run again and took a new route suggested by Defcon that morning. This process continued for the first week, and Tammy could see that she was making progress, having already lost 2 pounds, according to Defcon.

By the end of the second week, Tammy had lost 4 pounds, which means that she had earned $140 from her friends and family and another $140 in credit from her favorite department store (matching her friends' contributions), $20 in credit at her local grocery store, $20 in credit at the local sporting goods store, and 2,000 miles with her favorite airline. Tammy thought to herself that this whole diet thing was becoming quite a money maker!

Late in January, Tammy met with her friend Claire, the one getting married, and they went for a dress fitting. Tammy found that she fit well into a size 8 dress, but really wanted to wear a size 7. She made a notation in Diet Defcon about the dress and her desired size. Within minutes, she received a diet challenge from the dress shop where the fitting took place. If she lost the additional 10 pounds by the end of March, the dress shop would give her a 25 percent discount on the bridesmaid dress.

By mid-March, Tammy had reached 3.5 miles of running every morning, had lost 7 pounds, was eating a significantly more healthy diet, and generally felt much better about herself. Her doctor had sent her a note of encouragement, she received a $70 refund check from her health insurance company, and her pledges from friends and sponsor companies had increased to over $400! Defcon had entered her into a "biggest loser" contest against others with health profile and goals similar to hers, and she was presently running in 14th place out of over 200 people in her competition. She was hoping to move up in the standing, since the winner in each category received $1 for every pound lost by everyone in that category. That could easily add up to over $1,000!

By her goal date of April 15, Tammy had beat her goal of 15 pounds, having lost 18. She won the discount on her size 7 bridesmaid dress, had earned over $300 in food discounts, and had over $600 in pledges from friends and corporate sponsors. She finished her Defcon contest in third place, winning $.25 for every pound her cadre lost for a total of $315.75. Her picture and profile was displayed on Defcon's website, and she received a gift certificate for a new pair of running shoes from a popular sporting goods company.

Behind the Scenes

In this scenario, Tammy seeks help, guidance, and motivation in her effort to get in shape for her friend's wedding. By downloading an app by Diet Defcon, she received all of this and much more during the time that she's trying to lose weight. Let's look at what it took to keep her motivated and ultimately to productize her key life event.

DIET DEFCON: THE BUSINESS MODEL

Diet Defcon's business model is to act as a life-event hub, which seeks to support a consumer through a key life event using promotion, gamification, and rewards, both financial and otherwise. Diet Defcon earns revenue by capturing new customers for other companies (*quantafication, crowdsourcing, and cloudification*) and by prequalifying these customers to be targeted by these other companies for special promotions. Defcon arranges for customers to receive special discounts related to their needs (i.e., low-calorie foods, fitness equipment, motivational music) and receives a proportion of the value of the discounts as revenue (*contextification and crowdsourcing*). Diet Defcon also aggregates its customers in order to arrange reverse-Groupon auctions with which it secures additional discounts for its customers (*cloudification and crowdsourcing*). Finally, Diet Defcon is linked with the major healthcare insurance providers in the industry and arranges for health insurance discounts for people who participate in Defcon's weight loss programs (*contextification*).

STARTING A DIET WITH DIET DEFCON

Defcon asks for and typically receives access to certain personal health information from its members. This access is a requirement for participation, and most people volunteer their data to receive the benefits that Defcon provides. Once access is granted, Defcon downloads relevant data from the member's government-managed health profile, including such information as their historical weight, body mass index (BMI), blood pressure, blood glucose level, and cholesterol level, to develop a safe weight loss program for the individual member. Defcon also notifies the member's doctor of the recommended program and ensures that the member is healthy enough to proceed (*contextification*).

RUNNING ROUTE

Defcon knew Tammy's location based upon her smart phone and was able to map out an exercise route that would allow her to cover her target distance as safely as possible (*contextification*). Defcon tracked her pace when she exercised and also occasionally changed her route so that she wouldn't get bored. Had she chosen to, Defcon could have arranged for other people to join her when she ran, including setting the time and place for them to meet each morning.

EXERCISE PLAYLIST

When Defcon was installed on Tammy's phone, it scanned all of the music that she had on the phone. From this, Defcon was able to model her likes and dislikes, select those songs that she already owned that were upbeat and thus good choices to exercise to, and then made recommendations for further songs that she might like to purchase, based upon her preferences (*contextification and thingification*). While exercising, she was allowed to listen to partial clips of further recommended songs, and she could purchase them at a discount if she heard one that she liked.

FRIENDS AND FAMILY SPONSORSHIP

Using Tammy's Facebook and Twitter accounts, Defcon notified her friends and family that she is starting a diet and sought motivational messages from this audience to support her efforts (*socialfication and contextification*). Additionally, Defcon allows this audience to make pledges toward Tammy's goals. Pledges might be financial or nonfinancial, such as taking her to a movie or to a meal (*crowdsourcing*). These sponsors are kept up-to-date on Tammy's progress toward her goal, as her

Diet Defcon app on her smartphone is Bluetooth synched to her scales at home (*appification and thingification*).

SHOPPING WITH DEFCON

Using Tammy's weight goals and her health profile information, Defcon creates a daily menu for her to follow (*thingification and appification*). With her approval, Defcon then reaches out to the companies that produce the recommended foods and secures a range of coupons and other discounts for all of the items on her shopping list (*cloudification and crowdsourcing*). By using these coupons, Tammy is able to easily follow the recommended diet, while Defcon is able to show the participating vendors a direct benefit from the targeted discounts that they provided.

CORPORATE SPONSORSHIP

The companies providing discounts are also encouraged to provide financial sponsorship of Tammy's life event. Some will choose to pay cash for every pound that she loses. Others may provide further discounts on items that Tammy will need as she loses weight, such as new clothes and exercise gear (*contextification and socialfication*). Still others will chose to provide semi-monetary rewards along the way, such as bonus mileage in her frequent flyer program with her favorite airline. All of these rewards will be constantly monitored and updated, providing Tammy with strong positive feedback for her ongoing efforts.

DRESS DISCOUNT

The discount offered by the dress shop stemmed from a directed reverse auction set up by Defcon (*crowdsourcing*). Since Tammy's diet was tied to the wedding, which was called out on Tammy's personal calendar as well as her Facebook and

Twitter posts, Defcon knew to notify the dress shop of the opportunity to deal. As a result, Defcon secured the sponsored discount for Tammy before she began shopping for the dress with Claire (*socialfication, contextification, and crowdsourcing*). Once the auction had finished, Defcon directed Tammy to the correct store that offered the highest discount.

BIGGEST LOSER

Defcon gamified the dieting process by creating groups of participants with similar health profiles and similar weight loss goals. It then set them to compete with one another (*gamification*). Dozens or even hundreds of people competed with one another for who could lose the most weight in the specified time frame, and their weight loss would be sponsored by one or more corporate sponsors, such as exercise equipment companies, clothing brands, and other companies that might benefit from such sponsorship.

Scenario 3: Preparing for Midterms, Thursday, March 12, 2020

Juan awoke and quickly logged into his gmail account. He had sent his practice exam to his tutor, Syed, yesterday and was eager to see how well he had done. Syed was helping Juan with his applied statistics course, the capstone course in Juan's Data Sciences Bachelor's degree program at the University of Leeds. Sorting through the hundreds of emails he received overnight, Juan saw that he had not yet received a response from Syed, so he showered and walked down the street to grab a quick breakfast at IHOP. It was another sunny day in Southern California, and Juan enjoyed the mile walk to his "office" at his favorite restaurant.

Juan placed his order with his waiter. He then fired up his tablet computer and logged into QuantCorner app. Quant-Corner had sent Juan 15 new assignments that matched his knowledge and interests. Juan reviewed the specifications for each job while he ate his omelet. In particular, Juan focused on reading the specifications for a data modeling assignment from a Brazilian restaurant chain that was planning on opening a dozen new restaurants and was looking to determine the best locations within the major cities of Brazil.

Juan reviewed the sample data that the company provided, drew up some thoughts on the model that he might build to perform the sensitivity analysis, and came up with an estimate for how long he would need to complete the model, given that he had midterms over the next two weeks. He thought that he could complete the work within 20 hours during in a couple of days after midterms were over. He sent the company a quote for performing the analysis, and hoped that they'd accept and sign up with him within the next day or two.

Juan completed five more bids over breakfast, then packed up and returned home to study for his upcoming exam. While walking home, he received an email from Syed. Juan opened the video file in his iGlasses and listened to Syed's critique of the practice exam Juan completed the day before. Juan had missed a couple of nuances in the data that Syed had hoped he'd pick up on, and Syed provided some further pointers on how Juan could improve his performance on his upcoming midterm. Juan logged into his Cashbot account and sent a payment to Syed for his tutoring services.

When he got home, Juan launched his HelpMarket app and looked for tech support jobs he could pick up. He found one for a user having challenges with synching his iGlasses with his iPad10 through her cloud storage provider; something that Juan could explain how to fix in a couple of minutes. Juan created a short video describing the synching process and posted it to the site. The requester followed his guidance and about 15 minutes later she rated Juan's video as a five-star post. Juan checked his Cashbot account later in the day and found that he received a $5 payment from Apple for posting the support video. Over the course of the next year, he'd earn another $300 from that video from other users who took advantage of it.

Juan spent another two hours on HelpMarket, answering a range of user questions on technical products with which he was familiar. At the end of the session he rechecked his Cashbot balance, happy to see that it was again over $2,000 and over 10,000 points. The individual payments on Help-Market were small, but Juan had several hundred posts by now, each earning a little bit of income every week.

As a result, he'd have enough money to pay for his first semester of online MBA school at the Indian Institute of Management in Ahmedabad. Syed was trying to convince Juan to attend his alma mater, Lahore University of Management Sciences, but their online program wasn't as strong as IIM's and Juan wasn't interested in moving to Pakistan for two years for the onsite program, despite the internship offer from Syed's employer.

Finished with working for the day, Juan grabbed his iGlasses, launched his audible.com app, and listened to his homework reading while he went to the skate park down by the local high school. He'd skateboard for about an hour to blow off some steam and to study, then he would start working on the Brazilian analysis before dinner.

Another productive day.

Behind the Scenes

In this scenario, Juan has become a typical mobile, digital citizen of the 2020s. He's earning his degree online, while also earning a living one micropayment at a time. Let's look at how he's managed to create and support this lifestyle through the use of socialfication.

ONLINE EDUCATION

Juan is earning his college degree from a well-known university thousands of miles from his home in Southern California. By 2020, such distant learning will increasingly be the norm in our world, as universities open themselves up to the possibilities of socialfication, cloudification, and reaching out to ever-larger communities of students. Indeed, as I write this book, I am finishing my fourth year of online law school; and this is the second online degree program that I have attended in my career.

While there is some resistance to this epic change in how education is delivered as a service, this change will be inevitable, as more and more people around the globe enter the market for education as the primary tool for moving into the urbanized, globalized middle class. The top students in each country will be able to compete for the best jobs globally, while merely average students in the Western world will find it increasingly difficult to secure the best jobs in their own home countries, Globalization will continue its relentless homogenization of the world's market for human capital.

This effect will be most pronounced in those subject areas for which there are dramatic shortages of talent, such as data sciences. As such, there will be even greater demand for virtual education as a means to meet any unserved market demand as quickly as possible. Those universities that resist adopting this change will be at a significant disadvantage in the education market, as competition for the best students goes global. This is demonstrated by Juan's attendance at the University of Leeds, in the United Kingdom, which is on the other side of the planet from his home.

Finally, Juan is a "typical student" for the year 2020 in that he is a full time student who also works while studying. The cost of taking 4 to 10 years off work to earn one or more degrees is simply too high for most to afford. As a result, an ever-increasing proportion of students will be working while they are learning. This will also be true of older workers, who will find that they must retrain themselves one or more times in their careers in order to remain relevant to the ever-changing job market.

QUANTCORNER JOB BOARD

In this story, QuantCorner represents an online community that will be common by 2020. In this community, people with similar interests and backgrounds will not only interact with each other, they will form a marketplace for goods and services that the community can provide to potential customers (*socialfication, cloudification, and crowdsourcing*). Here, Quant-Corner has created a marketplace where companies needing the help of data scientists can post their jobs, and where data scientist members can bid to perform the work that has been posted (*cloudification, crowdsourcing, and gamification*). These marketplaces will be an advanced mash-up of Craigslist and eBay, and will allow companies to outsource specific chunks of work to a global marketplace of otherwise hard-to-find resources.

QuantCorner may also be viewed as a sort of monetized LinkedIn, where people can post their expertise and availability for work, and companies can identify resources who may be able to meet a specific need on a project or program in a competitive reverse-auction marketplace (*gamification, crowdsourcing, and cloudification*). Like all such marketplaces, QuantCorner is gamified, so that members like Juan can create and maintain an online reputation and score for the work that they perform; the better their results, the higher their community score, and hence the more in-demand they will be, and the more that they can charge for their services.

Companies that have cloudified their value chains will increasingly leverage online communities like QuantCorner to retain the services of rare and expensive resources, particularly those that are not readily available in the company's physical locations across the globe. Here, Juan represents a growing class of globalized, independent contractors who will capture an ever-growing proportion of high-value-added services across the world's labor markets.

HELPMARKET

HelpMarket is related to QuantCorner, but HelpMarket represents the low-end of the cloudified and socialfied value chain of work. HelpMarket is a place where people can post questions that they have, typically about a product or service that they have consumed, and will hopefully receive a good answer to their question by someone knowledgeable on the topic. When the questions posted are specifically tied to a vendor's product or service, that vendor can sponsor the question and provide a payment to whomever answers the customer's question. The answers provided are ranked by the person who asked the question (*gamification and socialfication*) and, the better the answer, the higher the potential payout by the sponsoring vendor.

Therefore, HelpMarket is a monetized mash-up of YouTube, Wikipedia, and the online support communities presently managed by a number of Fortune 1000 companies, like Microsoft. By plugging into the entire Internet user community, sponsoring companies can access a vastly greater range of contextual experts, that is, people who use their products or services in specific ways and, because of that experience, understand the potential shortcomings of these offerings and how to correct them (*gamification, cloudification, quantafication, and crowdsourcing*). Since the answers that are provided by the community compete with each other via gamification, only the best answers receive financial rewards at a greatly reduced unit cost to the sponsor.

For participants who create the best content, the answers may continue to generate revenues for months or years. Each time their content is used and scored, they receive a small payment from the content's sponsor. Naturally, the per-use payments will be quite small, but they will aggregate over time. For prolific and high-ranking participants on sites like HelpMarket, these payouts could become a significant portion of their annual income (*socialfication, cloudification, and crowdsourcing*).

Juan uses HelpMarket to add to his income from his online activities. He jealously manages and protects his online rankings, as these directly impact his income potential and also represent scores that are at least as important to his career as his college grades. By dedicating an hour or two every day to HelpMarket, Juan has created both an annuity stream of income and measurable evidence of his ability to solve other peoples' problem.

CASHBOT AND SECONDARY MARKETS

CashBot is Juan's preferred online microeconomy, where he conducts the bulk of his personal money management. As one of the follow-ons to PayPal, CashBot automates the process of sending and receiving payments, particularly in a mobile world. What makes CashBot different is its extremely low per-transaction cost, which encourages micropayments, and its operating headquarters in a third world country with little or no financial services regulations and less-than-friendly relationships with the tax authorities of most of the world's countries.

Further, CashBot allows users to transact either in national currencies, like dollars, euros, and yuans, or in CashBot "points," which can be used as a neutral currency of sorts within the CashBot marketplace. Since these points are effectively used to barter for goods and services within CashBot, they don't directly translate into local currencies and, thus, are extremely difficult to tax. CashBot maintains an ongoing analysis of the "value" of CashBot points based upon the sorts of barter deals made within the marketplace. This allows users to keep track of the apparent value of their points. Working off of trends like those that created the golddigging described in Chapter 15, CashBot facilitates the creation of frictionless markets that are free of government control.

CashBot's success has been based on the combination of low barriers to entry by participants, the transparency that it provides to these participants, and the invisibility to national governments of the transactions that CashBot facilitates. Cash-

Bot, and others like it, looks to becoming a global economic powerhouse. While its current marketplace only represents an estimated one percent of global GDP, CashBot is more than doubling its transactions of currency and points every year.

With CashBot and marketplaces like QuantCorner and HelpMarket, the control that nations have over their own economies is beginning to erode. These marketplaces are in the cloud; they are nowhere and everywhere, and the markets that they support are likewise beyond the reach of most national governments. People like Juan are able to participate without worrying about work permits, visas, banking accounts, or payroll taxes, and are able to take advantage of merit-based, frictionless labor markets. Cashbot drives governments crazy, but it is so compelling, popular, and prolific that there is little that governments can do to slow down the migration of their economies into these socialified, cloudified markets.

Scenario 4: Tax Time in America, Monday, February 3, 2020

Doug walked down the street near his office trying to select the best place to stop for a quick lunch. His Galaxy S10 glasses pointed out several options, and he finally chose the Laotian restaurant at the corner (*thingification and contextification*). As he sat down and began to review the menu, his glasses chimed at the arrival of a new email. Normally, he'd instruct his glasses to file the email away until he finished his lunch, but this one was from the IRS, and he had previously instructed his glasses to notify him when his tax information arrived. So, this message got through his inbox filter (*contextification and thingification*).

The email opened in his field of view, and Doug saw the summary of his 1040 federal tax return form. The form was precompleted by the IRS and was ready for Doug's review and approval. As Doug ate his lunch, he read through the tax form, seeing that it correctly incorporated his various deductions, including his mortgage, his student loan expenses from his Master's program, even his predicted state income and sales tax payments. Doug noted that the sales tax estimate only included purchases on Amazon, eBay, and TechGlobe, but didn't include the tax paid on his new car.

Doug quickly accessed his personal accounting app, found the tax payment on the car, and added it to the amount shown on his tax form (*appification and cloudification*). He reviewed the other entries from the IRS, and everything looked appropriate. Doug had signed up for audit assistance insurance with Quicken, due to his home office deduction, so he forwarded the file to his assigned accountant, as his insurance contract required, and waited for her approval (*cloudification, quantafication, and crowdsourcing*).

The next day, Doug received an email from his accountant who had reviewed the tax forms and found them to be accurate. Doug then approved the forms and sent them on to the IRS. The following morning, his refund appeared in his primary checking account. He noted the extra $50 for filing early and the extra $100 for filing electronically. His return wasn't as much as it used to be, but it was nice to have a little extra cash nonetheless.

With his federal returns completed, he could now complete his state returns, which still had to be submitted by mail. Perhaps in another couple of years the state would finally catch up and precomplete its own tax submission. The law had been passed two years before, but the state's system had been hacked and officials had to take it offline while attempts were made to close the vulnerabilities that the hackers had found. Quicken had already completed the necessary forms and showed that Doug owed the state a further $500, despite the car sales tax deduction. Oh well, easy come, easy go.

Behind the Scenes

This scenario portrays a situation that is a long time in coming. Other countries, such as Norway, already follow the approach of precompleting taxpayer returns, as a matter of both convenience and accuracy. Once the payer has reviewed the forms, and either approved them as is or made any necessary corrections, the taxes are approved and the process is completed.

The U.S. government has allowed electronic filing for some time now, but it has not taken the step to proactively complete tax returns on the payee's behalf. Due to the deep financial troubles that had befallen the country during the Great Recession, protecting the national revenue stream became a matter of national security. After all, without bucks, there can be no bullets. Thus, the government finally passed a tax reform law that both simplified and automated the majority of the tax collection process.

ELECTRONIC TAX FORM

There is nothing new about electronic tax submission, but what is new in this scenario is that the government prepopulates all of the relevant data at its disposal, which is the vast majority of what is required from the taxpayer. The major items to include, such as income and deductions, are already known to our financial institutions and local governments; the information simply needs to be submitted to the federal government in a form that it could use.

Where additions had to be made, such as a home office deduction, once the taxpayer incorporated this into his or her return, the government could keep track of this addition and keep the deduction on file for as long as the situation remained. This was all possible back in the late 1990s, but it took the risk of the government defaulting on its debt to force the reform act that finally automated the revenue collection process.

REAL-TIME AUDITING

By having the vast majority of U.S. taxpayers complete their forms electronically, cost of operating the IRS was greatly reduced. The department let go thousands of clerks who had previously supported the manual processing of tax returns and also greatly improved the audit process. In effect, any return that was not edited by the taxpayer would automatically pass an automated audit. More than ninety percent of tax returns never required further review (*accelerate and data enable*). Those that did require review first went through several layers of intelligent analysis, during which the government looked at all of the taxpayers spending habits through the year and could paint a pretty accurate picture of each person's actual financial situation almost immediately (*contextification*). Any peculiarities were immediately identified by the intelligent audit systems and could be resolved almost immediately by electronic agents that would further investigate any issues.

AUDIT PROTECTION

Firms that previously were in the business of helping taxpayers complete their taxes needed to adapt quickly to the changes in the tax process, and most moved into the business of audit insurance (*cloudification and crowdsourcing*). Since the government's ability to properly track peoples' income and spending was dramatically improved, those who had exceptions to report to the government tended to fall under tremendous scrutiny. Support by tax professionals was critical to get an additional deduction through the process and to avoid the substantial penalties associated with any unsupportable deduction. Nevertheless, those companies that previously supported tax reporting saw their business fall to a trickle of what it used to be under the old tax process.

AUTOMATED VERSUS MANUAL PROCESSING

Once the government formalized the automated submission of tax returns, it could put a price on the time value of money, as well as that for accepting the physical submission of tax forms. Thus, any taxpayer who submitted taxes early received a tax credit, while anyone who needed to submit taxes in a physical format had to pay a significant penalty and were far more likely to be audited.

SALES TAX

As more and more consumers moved to online purchases, it was inevitable that the government would begin to tax the resulting revenues. Online retailers lobbied hard and long against these taxes, but the government revenue crisis made the application of these taxes inevitable. It was a simple matter for these organizations to both collect these taxes and to submit the necessary information to the government.

The challenge was to capture all of the information from the thousands of retailers around the globe. As these tax rules came into being, many consumers moved to offshore retailers who chose to not participate in the U.S. government's program. Further, an entire industry quickly formed that allowed consumers to make purchases while remaining anonymous, sheltering their purchases from government scrutiny. Thus began a game of cat and mouse involving billions of dollars of potential tax revenues that the federal government desperately wanted to get its hands on.

Scenario 5: An Apple (Or Google) a Day Keeps the Doctor Away, Thursday, July 16, 2020

After she and her husband had been trying for a few months, Sarah's ob/gyn notified her that she was eight weeks pregnant. He asked if she wanted to have a comprehensive screening performed on her fetus and if she'd like to have her baby's genome mapped. Her screening was covered by her insurance, but the genome map would cost $500. Sarah recognized the benefit of having the map available for her baby's future, so she signed up for the procedure. She came back the following week and the doctor took the baby's DNA sample, sending it off to the lab for decoding.

Two weeks later the results of the screening came back, and Sarah was relieved to find out that her daughter proved to be free of the genetic defects responsible for over 2,500 diseases. Genomisys, the company that performed the analysis, offered to both store the genetic sequence information and also to store the cord blood from Sarah's daughter after the birth, both at a discount if Sarah allowed her daughter's genome information to be used as part of its growing database of individual genomes. The discount was worth several hundred dollars, and Sarah saw the benefit of storing the cord blood for her daughter's future health needs, so she signed up for both deals and thought no more about it for several weeks.

About a month later, Sarah received an email from Genomisys, notifying her that they had studied her baby's genome in more detail and that her daughter's genome had several single-nucleotide polymorphisms (SNPs) that Genomisys had been studying for their potential role in a range of diseases. Because Sarah's daughter had these SNPs and Genomisys already had her genome on file, she was an ideal candidate to contribute to a long-term study related to SNPs and their role in causing disease. If Sarah agreed to her daughter's participation in the study, Genomisys would cover the costs of storing the baby's cord blood and would also pay for a significant proportion of the baby's health-care costs through her first 18 years. Given the ever-increasing cost of health care, Sarah agreed to participate in the study.

When Shelly was born, the doctors collected the blood from her umbilical cord and sent it to Genomisys for long-term storage. Sarah and Tom were thrilled to be parents and were happy that they had signed up with Genomisys. By 2020, it had already become clear that there were going to be huge breakthroughs in human health management coming from genetic mapping, and Shelly stood to benefit from these advances as a participant in the studies.

Shelly's early childhood was pretty normal. Sarah and Tom received typical pediatric care notifications for checkups and immunizations on their smart phones. Their phones would automatically look for openings in her doctor's calendar that matched their availability. Their car would notify the doctor's receptionist when they were on their way to their appointment, allowing the doctor to maximize her patient load and utilization each day while minimizing the patients' wait times.

By 2020, common childhood ailments such as the cold, the flu, and chicken pox, could be checked with saliva monitors that plug into a smart phone's ear jack, just like credit card scanners from the previous decade. Have the child lick a small plastic stick, plug the stick into the disposable measuring unit and within five seconds you'd know if the child had caught something. When there was a positive signal, a note would automatically be sent to the pediatrician who could email back a treatment regiment and perform ongoing monitoring while the child recovered. Shelly had the typical bumps, bruises, and fevers of any young kid, and all seemed totally normal, until her tenth birthday.

By this time, 2030, the genetic analysts at Genomisys had developed meaningful evidence that the interesting SNPs that they had found in Shelly's genome were now believed to be linked to a late-onset kidney disease that leads to kidney failure by the patient's mid-40s. There appeared to be a 50 to 80 percent correlation, but a direct connection had yet to be determined. The doctors, data scientists, and geneticists were maturing their data on how the target SNPs were activated and were then tied to kidney function, but since the disease was one of late-onset, they needed more monitoring of people as they aged. Shelly's parents were asked to allow her to participate in the ongoing life study, for which she would receive payment and additional healthcare services. They agreed. The doctors and scientists wanted to monitor the levels of various proteins in Sally's blood and urine over the course of her life, as well as keep a general health diary for her. She was given a smart phone with several apps that assisted in monitoring her activity, diet, and general wellbeing. It also had sensors that when attached would monitor critical protein levels through her saliva and a remote monitor that would check her urine when she used the toilet. All of this was largely unobtrusive to

Shelly; using the apps and the sensors became integrated into her daily life.

By 2050, when Shelly reached the age of 30, there were clear signs that her kidneys were beginning to degenerate. They had only lost a percentage or two of their function, but the trend was definitely showing up in the daily monitoring. Using the data that had been collected thus far, doctors had largely determined the mechanisms of the disease and various therapies were being identified to slow down its progress.

Still, by 2065, it was clear that therapeutics would not be enough to prevent Shelly's kidneys from failing by the age of 55. In fact, she'd suffer significant impairment by the age of 50.

As such, Shelly elected to have replacement surgery when she was 45 years old; this decision was supported by the life-cycle cost analysis performed by her insurer. Stem cells were extracted from her stored cord blood and the offending SNPs were genetically altered to fix the encoding error. Several of the corrected cells were put back into cryogenic storage, so that they would be available later. The remainder of the cells went to company BioSyn in India, where they were used to grow two new kidneys in its bioreactors.

Three months later, the kidneys had passed all of their functional tests and were ready for implantation. Shelly was admitted to the Gates Memorial Hospital in New York where she was prepped for surgery. Her doctor, Dr. Kellogg, logged into the surgical simulator in his office in San Juan, Costa Rica, established the data link to the robotic surgery table at Sinai, and performed a flawless implant of Susan's new kidneys over the course of the next four hours.

Shelly recovered within a couple of weeks, and tests confirmed that her new kidneys were working perfectly. Further, the altered SNPs were not causing rejection problems with her immune system. Within a month, she was good as new, and lived out the remainder of her life without worrying about her kidneys.

Behind the Scenes

In this scenario, Shelly's parents become early adopters of genomics, the data science behind analyzing and understanding the information encoded in DNA. Their foresight paid off for Shelly, as it allowed for the early diagnosis and eventual cure of a genetically based disease that she was born with. Let's take a deeper look at what took place behind the scenes in this story.

AUTOMATIC SCHEDULING

To anyone using a smart phone today, this advancement in the healthcare industry in the United States is sorely needed. Scheduling seems to be the most difficult task faced by health-care administrators, and yet most of us are very comfortable using the automated calendaring functions provided by our smart phones. Within a few years, it is very likely that someone will look to simplify this problem for this industry, and there may well "be an app for that" in the near future. For most of us, it will be none too soon (*appification and contextification*).

GENOME MAPPING

Genomics is advancing far faster than Moore's law. While genomic mapping of an individual cost in excess of $500,000 in 2009, by 2012 this price had fallen to under $10,000. By the late 2010s, the price should fall to significantly less than $1,000. However, while the price of mapping has fallen substantially, the cost of storing these maps is still nontrivial. Each genome requires approximately three gigabytes of storage space, so to store the genomes of millions of people will require exabytes of storage. Further, to analyze all of this data across millions of genome data files will be a huge challenge to the "Big Data" scientist. However, innovation in this space is almost assured, because the potential benefits, and profits are almost incalculable (*data enable*).

DISEASE DIAGNOSIS

While using genomic analysis to find disease, vectors will provide a great benefit to our collective health, as we are still developing our understanding of how our DNA works and how different genes are expressed throughout a person's lifetime. While scientists recognize that certain gene or genetic segments (SNPs) are related to certain types of disease, the exact mechanisms involved remain elusive. By analyzing the ongoing biology of people who carry interesting SNPs, scientist may be able to develop a deep understanding of how each SNP impacts the health of the carrier. This will necessitate constant monitoring of the individual's health, which means that this monitoring must be made as unobtrusive as possible (*contextification and appification*).

Much like present-day monitoring of blood sugar for diabetics, participants in these studies will keep track of key bodily metrics on an ongoing basis. This data will be integrated with the subject's genetic characteristics, cross-compared with results from other subjects, and feed biological models that slowly reveal how our bodies work in minute detail. This whole process will require the collection and analysis of truly gargantuan amounts of data and the datafication of daily routines of the participants in these life-long studies (*contextification, appification, and cloudification*).

ORGAN MANUFACTURING

With sufficient understanding of the human genome and the functions played by stem cells in the growth of unique tissues in our bodies (like individual organs), it is likely that organ manufacturing will be a reality by the middle of this century. Organs will be made from stem cells taken from the target patient, ensuring that the new organ is not rejected by the subject's immune system. Further, known genetic defects in the patient's genome may be corrected at the start of the growth process, correcting for potential problems in the organ's long-term use by the patient.

The creation of new organs will require mapping of existing organs to ensure that they are producing physically exact copies of the existing organ. This will require frequent, repetitive imaging by Magnetic Resonance Imaging (MRI) machines or other similar imaging technologies. In turn, these images will need to be analyzed and stored, adding still more data to the process described in this scenario.

While this scenario may seem to come from a Hollywood movie, every technology and technique described here is under active development by the medical industry. Progress in each of these scientific fields is being made in leaps and bounds. As such, I'm confident that our ability to realize a scenario such as the one presented will be almost assured in the time frames used.

NOTES

Introduction

1. www.cisco.com/en/US/solutions/collateral/ns341/ns525/ns537/ns705/ns827/white_paper_c11-520862.html
2. www.aiim.org/pdfdocuments/Rise-of-the-Information-Professional-White-Paper.pdf

Chapter 1

1. www.nielsen.com/us/en/newswire/2013/mobile-majority—u-s—smartphone-ownership-tops-60-.html
2. pewinternet.org/Reports/2013/in-store-mobile-commerce.aspx
3. www.mmaglobal.com/research/mobile-advertising-trends-2011
4. www.idc.com/getdoc.jsp?containerId=prUS24302813
5. www.itu.int/en/ITU-D/Statistics/Documents/facts/ICTFactsFigures2013.pdf
6. www.itu.int/pub/D-IND-ICTOI-2012
7. www.idc.com/getdoc.jsp?containerId=prUS24302813
8. news.bbc.co.uk/2/hi/business/1102798.stm
9. web.lib.hse.fi/FI/yrityspalvelin/pdf/2000/Enokia.pdf; i.nokia.com/blob/view/-/2268488/data/3/-/NSN-form-2013.pdf; us.blackberry.com/content/dam/bbCompany/Desktop/Global/PDF/Investors/Documents/2000/2000rim_ar.pdf; us.blackberry.com/content/dam/bbCompany/Desktop/Global/PDF/Investors/Documents/2012/2012rim_ar_40F.pdf
10. www.cdc.gov/nchs/data/nhis/earlyrelease/wireless201212.pdf
11. files.ctia.org/pdf/CTIA_Survey_YE_2012_Graphics-FINAL.pdf
12. files.ctia.org/pdf/CTIA_Survey_YE_2012_Graphics-FINAL.pdf
13. files.ctia.org/pdf/CTIA_Survey_YE_2012_Graphics-FINAL.pdf
14. files.ctia.org/pdf/CTIA_Survey_YE_2012_Graphics-FINAL.pdf
15. files.ctia.org/pdf/CTIA_Survey_YE_2012_Graphics-FINAL.pdf
16. www.apple.com/pr/library/2013/01/07App-Store-Tops-40-Billion-Downloads-with-Almost-Half-in-2012.html
17. investor.apple.com/secfiling.cfm?filingID=1193125-12-444068; investor.google.com/pdf/2012_google_annual_report.pdf

18. www.gartner.com/newsroom/id/1529214
19. www.adeven.com/downloads/08_12_press_release-apptrace_eng.pdf
20. marketinfogroup.com/downloads/Location_Based_Services_Market_Tech
    nology_Outlook_TOC.pdf

Chapter 2

1. investor.fb.com/secfiling.cfm?filingID=1326801-13-3
2. investor.fb.com/secfiling.cfm?filingID=1326801-13-3
3. www.experian.com/blogs/marketing-forward/2012/05/16/15-stats-about
   -facebook/
4. https://blog.twitter.com/en-gb/2013/twitter7
5. https://blog.twitter.com/en-gb/2013/twitter7
6. engineering.twitter.com/2011/05/engineering-behind-twitters-new-search.html
7. twittercounter.com/pages/100, Accessed March 2013
8. articles.philly.com/2010-07-12/news/24967905_1_facebook-popular-social
   -networking-website-divorce-case
9. investor.fb.com/secfiling.cfm?filingID=1326801-13-3
10. investor.fb.com/secfiling.cfm?filingID=1326801-13-3
11. investor.fb.com/secfiling.cfm?filingID=1326801-13-3

Chapter 3

1. phx.corporate-ir.net/phoenix.zhtml?c=97664&p=irol-reportsannual
2. www.walmartstores.com/sites/annual-report/2012/
3. www.walmartstores.com/sites/annual-report/2012/
4. ir.jcpenney.com/phoenix.zhtml?c=70528&p=irol-reportsannual
5. www.searsholdings.com/invest/docs/SHC_2012_Form_10-K.pdf#pagemode
   =thumbs&page=1&zoom=100,0,0; ir.jcpenney.com/phoenix.zhtml?c=70528
   &p=irol-reportsannual; services.corporate-ir.net/SEC.Enhanced/SecCapsule
   .aspx?c=94746&fid=8641140; www.barnesandnobleinc.com/for_investors/annual
   _reports/2012_bn_annual_report.pdf
6. files.shareholder.com/downloads/AMDA-E2NTR/2710062337x0x659407/925
   BA93A-91ED-4935-A1E6-16EA88694410/2012_Annual_Report.pdf
7. files.shareholder.com/downloads/AMDA-E2NTR/2710062337x0x659407/925
   BA93A-91ED-4935-A1E6-16EA88694410/2012_Annual_Report.pdf
8. www.internetretailer.com/2012/06/14/global-e-commerce-sales-will-top
   -125-trillion-2013

Chapter 4

1. www.youtube.com/yt/press/statistics.html
2. www.youtube.com/yt/press/statistics.html
3. www.youtube.com/yt/press/statistics.html

4. articles.latimes.com/2012/may/24/entertainment/la-et-ct-idolfinale-20120524
5. www.youtube.com/yt/press/statistics.html
6. investor.apple.com/secfiling.cfm?filingID=1193125-12-444068 investor.google
   .com/pdf/2012_google_annual_report.pdf
7. money.cnn.com/2010/02/02/news/companies/napster_music_industry/
8. www.ifpi.org/content/section_resources/dmr2013.html
9. www.scmagazine.com/2013-mobile-device-survey/slideshow/1222/
10. www.naa.org/Trends-and-numbers/newspaper-Revenue/newspaper-media
    -Industry-Revenue-Profile-2012.aspx
11. www.theesa.com/facts/pdfs/esa_essential_facts_2010.pdf
12. www.bloomberg.com/news/2011-02-23/global-box-office-sales-rose-8-in
    -2010-to-record-31-8-billion.html
13. blogs.wsj.com/digits/2011/04/07/selling-virtual-game-winnings-a-3-billion
    -industry/
14. www.cisco.com/en/US/solutions/collateral/ns341/ns525/ns537/ns705/ns827/
    white_paper_c11-520862.html

Chapter 5

1. royal.pingdom.com/2012/01/17/internet-2011-in-numbers/
2. www.forbes.com/sites/joemckendrick/2013/02/20/cloud-computing-boosts
   -next-generation-of-startups-survey-shows/
3. www.forbes.com/sites/joemckendrick/2013/02/20/cloud-computing-boosts
   -next-generation-of-startups-survey-shows/
4. www.microsoft.com/en-us/news/features/2012/mar12/03-05cloudcomputing
   jobs.aspx

Chapter 6

1. Corporate Usage Statistics, 2012, Facebook.com
2. www.mckinsey.com/insights/business_technology/big_data_the_next_frontier
   _for_innovation
3. https://corporate.target.com/_media/TargetCorp/annualreports/content/
   download/pdf/Annual-Report.pdf;   media.corporate-ir.net/media_files/
   irol/65/65828/reports/2002_TGT_annual_HTML/index2.htm

Chapter 7

1. www.mobilemarketer.com/cms/news/research/11974.html

Chapter 8

1. investor.fb.com/secfiling.cfm?filingID=1326801-13-3
2. www.businessinsider.com/jared-fogles-subway-diet-15-years-later-2013-6
3. en.wikipedia.org/wiki/Main_Page Accessed September 2013

Chapter 9

1. Source: New York Stock Exchange Historical Data

Chapter 10

1. investor.apple.com/secfiling.cfm?filingID=1193125-12-444068 investor.google
   .com/pdf/2012_google_annual_report.pdf

Chapter 11

1. www.gartner.com/newsroom/id/1862714
2. www.huffingtonpost.com/tag/bank-layoffs Accessed March 2013
3. www.salesforce.com/company/investor/financials.jsp

Chapter 14

1. www.walmartstores.com/sites/annual-report/2012/
2. www.rovio.com/en/mobile-news/284/rovio-entertainment-reports-2012
   -financial-results
3. investor.apple.com/secfiling.cfm?filingID=1193125-12-444068
4. investor.apple.com/secfiling.cfm?filingID=1193125-12-444068

Chapter 15

1. www.aiim.org/pdfdocuments/IW_Big-Data_2012.pdf
2. www.eweek.com/database/ibm-big-data-analytics-to-drive-20b-in-revenue
   -by-2015/

Chapter 17

1. www.businessinsider.com/morgan-stanley-ecommerce-disruption-2013
   -1?op=1
2. www.comscore.com/Insights/Presentations_and_Whitepapers/2013/2013
   _Mobile_Future_in_Focus

Chapter 18

1. www.alsbridge.com/news/2013-benchmark-survey-results

INDEX